The Plowman Sings

The Essential Fiction, Poetry, and Drama of America's Forgotten Regionalist Jay G. Sigmund

Edited by
Zachary Michael Jack

University Press of America,® Inc.
Lanham · Boulder · New York · Toronto · Plymouth, UK

Copyright © 2008 by
University Press of America,® Inc.
4501 Forbes Boulevard
Suite 200
Lanham, Maryland 20706
UPA Acquisitions Department (301) 459-3366

Estover Road
Plymouth PL6 7PY
United Kingdom

All rights reserved
Printed in the United States of America
British Library Cataloging in Publication Information Available

Library of Congress Control Number: 2008931043
ISBN-10: 0-7618-4282-9 (paperback : alk. paper)
ISBN-13: 978-0-7618-4282-8 (paperback : alk. paper)
eISBN-10: 0-7618-4285-3
eISBN-13: 978-0-7618-4285-9

∞™ The paper used in this publication meets the minimum
requirements of American National Standard for Information
Sciences—Permanence of Paper for Printed Library Materials,
ANSI Z39.48—1984

Contents

Editor's Preface	vii
Acknowledgments	ix
America's Forgotten Regionalist, Jay G. Sigmund An Essay by Editor Zachary Michael Jack	1

I. Fiction

From *Wapsipinicon Tales* (Prairie Publishing Company, 1927)
The Foot Hoe	18

From *Merged Blood* (Maizeland Press, 1929)
Dubbing Season	21
The Way Out	26

From *The Ridge Road*, 1930 (Prairie Publishing Company, 1930)
Puddles	30
The Runaway	35
Bitter Herbs	39

From *The Least of These*, 1935 (Prairie Press, 1935)
The Old Order Changeth	45
Old Aches and Bloody Claws	49

II. Poetry

From *Frescoes* (B.J. Brimmer Company, 1922)
Birds of Prey	54
A White Pigeon	55
The Folk Dancer	56
Ego	56
The Cardinal	57
The Etcher	58
The Minister's Wife	59

From *Pinions* (James T. White & Co., 1923)
Crows	61
The Mystic River-pool	61
My Neighbor	62
Bewilderment	63
Rubbish	63

Contents

Tempted	64
The Wanderer	65
Souls	65
Failures	66
A Gray-haired Bard Speaks	67
Genus Homo	68

From *Land o' Maize Folk* (James T. White & Co., 1924)

To A Fish Hawk	68
Open Season	69
A Maize Country Pioneer's Interment	69
Maize Country Natal Day	71
Forecast	72
Pastoral	72
A Plowman Sings	73
Autumn Nocturne, Maize Village Grocery Store	74

From *Drowsy Ones* (Prairie Publishing Company, 1925)

Retired	75
Visitor	76
Surcease	76
Hill Soul's Death	77
Prairie Bachelor	77

From *The Ridge Road* (Prairie Publishing Company, 1930)

Grubber's Day	78
Landlocked Sailor	79
Taxidermist	80
To a Wounded Mallard in Midwinter	81
Hooked Rug	81
Ridge Road Wife's Holiday	82
The Younger Ridge Road Men	83
Hill Spinster's Sunday	83
Loam-Wounded	84
Second Marriage	85

From *Burroak and Sumac* (Cornell College, 1936)

Soliloquy on a River Road	87
Old Men in Gardening Time	88
Corn Belt Metropolis Notable	88
Masters of Old Matsell Farm	89
Hill Woman's Dream After Drought	89
Herb Doctor	90
Firstborn	91
Drunken Landowner	92

Contents v

Weather Prophet 92
Mass for a Tenant Farmer 93
Husker 94

From *Heron at Sunset* (Cornell College, 1938)
Rug Hooker 94
Asylum Dance 95
Octogenarian 96
False Prophets 96
Night Musings 97
Heron at Sunset 97

From *The Hawk That Haunts the Sky* (Coe College, 1937)
Sunday 98
Morning Mists on the Wapsipinicon 98

III: Drama

Folk Stuff (Samuel French, 1937) 102

Index 119
About the Editor 121

Editor's Preface

Had Jay G. Sigmund dropped a poem in a bottle in the waters of his beloved Wapsipinicon River before his premature death in 1937, it might well have washed up on my Wapsie River-bordering farm. Little more than thirty miles and seventy years, as the river flows, separate us—I at my desk looking out on the hills of Grant Wood country; Sigmund, in memory, on the shores of the Wapsie as it flows past his hometown of Waubeek, Iowa, just upriver from here. Jay Sigmund and I grow from the same soil, draw from the same well.

I discovered the forgotten work of Jay G. Sigmund as one chances on a sepia photo of a lost grandfather. Something about Sigmund's beamish eyes and his open, moony face struck me familiar. Something about his work—its plainspoken poetry, its careful chiaroscuro, its sweet sadness—I am predisposed to admire. In it eddies the masterful midwestern currents I already know: Sherwood Anderson, Edgar Lee Masters, and Carl Sandburg, to name a few. And yet it is inimitable, shaped by corn country wind, water, and weather—what the French call *terrior*, a word for which we Anglophones have no adequate translation but which signifies something vital, and indivisible: the smallest patch of earth from which a crop, be it vine, branch, or person, grows. It's that peculiar hillside, hillock, and humus that ripens the grape which makes the wine that tastes like no other. It's that singular milieu which feeds and quenches the writer who fleshes and sweetens the book.

Jay Sigmund had the kind of face one warmed to in an instant, the face of a gentleman farmer or doctor, a favorite teacher or loyal high school chum. He had a straight-shooting insurance man's face in the days when an insurance agent was part minister, part mayor, and part medic, in any case woven into the fabric of the community whose wealth and safety it was his business to safeguard. But Sigmund's visage was also, and tellingly, a writer's, though it escaped the telltale worry lines and darkened brow. Indeed, Sigmund's greatest gift may have been how he managed, in an area of celebrated author suicides, dust-ups, and crack-ups, on one hand, and drunken, anti-social, and downright ugly behavior on the other, to lead a "normal" life that just happened to be literary. In the process, he earned the respect of an impossibly eclectic "clientele" that included world-famous artists, hard-nosed literary critics, savvy Cedar Rapids, Iowa businessmen, farmers and neighbors, and the thousands of clients in Iowa and Minnesota especially whose insurance needs he served.

Whether Jay Sigmund will ever again realize the literary reputation he enjoyed in the Roaring Twenties is a question as unanswerable as it is compelling. The emerging field of place studies must have time to blossom and bear fruit. But I have a notion as inexorable as Jay Sigmund's Wapsipinicon that his name will again be known—not in the garish light of writerly celebrity but in the reflective, temperate hue of the waters upon which his spirit moves.

Acknowledgments

Many thanks to Jay G. Sigmund's longtime employer, Minnesota Mutual Life, now Securian Financial, for supporting this volume. Special acknowledgement belongs to Margaret Jensen for her advocacy, wisdom, and vision.

Work appearing in this volume has been altered as little as possible to conform to standards of contemporary usage. Exclamation marks, used liberally in the original after the poetic fashion of the day, have been replaced with periods where appropriate. Similarly, as a general rule, periods have been substituted for overabundant semi-colons.

The editor wishes to thank Samuel French, Inc. for the right to reprint *Folk Stuff* by Jay G. Sigmund and Betty Smith. Copyright 1937 by Samuel French. Copyright 1965 by Betty Smith. Reprint rights by special arrangement with Samuel French, Inc.

Samuel French requires the inclusion of the following caution notice:

CAUTION: Professional and amateurs are hereby warned that *Folk Stuff* being fully protected under the copyright laws of the United States of America, the British Commonwealth countries, including Canada, and other countries of the Copyright Union, is subject to royalty. All rights, including professional, amateur, motion picture, recitation, public reading, radio, television and cable broadcasting, and the rights of translation into foreign languages, are strictly reserved. Any inquiry regarding the availability of performance rights, or the purchase of individual copies of the authorized acting edition, must be directed to Samuel French Inc., 45 West 25 Street, NY, NY 10010 with other locations in Hollywood and Toronto, Canada.

America's Forgotten Regionalist: Jay G. Sigmund

Every midwestern state in Jazz-Age America, it seemed, claimed a Jay Sigmund—a native son or daughter who, against steepest odds, made it big in the world of arts and letters. Just south and west of Jay Sigmund's Iowa, Maryville, Missouri touted farm-born Homer Croy, who went from the University of Missouri directly to a prolific publishing career in New York and Hollywood. To the east of Sigmund's Iowa, Galesburg, Illinois boasted Carl Sandburg, whose writerly flame was lit at Lombard College, stoked by a brief stint at the *Chicago Daily News*, and later continued in Michigan and in North Carolina, from whence Sandburg earned two Pulitzer Prizes. East of Sandburg's Illinois, the pride of Camden, Ohio—bestselling author Sherwood Anderson—left his home state at first opportunity, moving to Chicago, New Orleans, and, finally, to Virginia. Considered collectively, these peripatetic authorial lives confirm a midwestern pattern: the great author receives his or her education, leaves home, writes about home from afar, and returns, if at all, in ashes.

Happily, Jay G. Sigmund (1885–1937), arguably Iowa's greatest writer of the Regionalist movement, broke the mold not simply by writing about home, but by staying at home in Cedar Rapids, Iowa. That a home place could be the continual wellspring of one's art rather than an impediment to it was Sigmund's greatest rallying cry. Writing in 1929, the beginning of Sigmund's national fame, Carl Sandburg praised the literary revolution begun by Sigmund and his fellow Iowa Regionalists in his weekly column "From the Notebook of Carl Sandburg" in the *Chicago Daily News*. In what amounted to an argument for staying put, Sandburg proclaimed, "In other words, Iowa is humanly as tragic and mysterious with the fate of man as was Greece, Rome, and the soils that produced the cultures of the Elizabethan or the Victorian eras."

Carl Sandburg was one of Sigmund's many champions. H. L. Mencken, Sherwood Anderson, and Ilya Tolstoy, among others, all corresponded with him. California poet Robinson Jeffers lauded Sigmund's "fine powers of imagination and imaginative sympathy, as well as musical verse." A truly national rather than merely regional author, Sigmund earned his first *New York Times* review for just his second full-length book of poetry, 1923's *Pinions*, of which the *Times* reviewer opined, "To say that they [the poems] are somewhat in the vein of Edgar Lee Masters is not to suggest imitation, for they are fresh and original both in content and in rendering." When, building on the success of his poetry, Sigmund turned to fiction in the late 1920s, his efforts likewise garnered immediate positive notice. Editors tapped his short fiction not only for the prestigious Best Short Stories series, but also for numerous anthologies, including *The American Caravan*, where his work appeared beside Ernest Hemingway's and Gertrude Stein's. Unbelievably, in 1930 alone, Boston editor Edward J. O'Brien listed six Sigmund shorts as among the best short stories of that year.

And yet for all these achievements, Jay Sigmund has been all but forgotten by contemporary literary scholars, despite authoring, in just sixteen years, according to Sigmund biographer Edward Ferreter, over 1200 poems, 125 short stories, 25 one-act plays, one three-act play, and one unpublished novel, *Purple Washboards*, while simultaneously working full-time as an insurance executive. To remedy this neglect is the raison d'être of this collection, *The Plowman Sings*—the first Sigmund anthology ever to include the author's work across three genres and the first widely available compendium of his work in nearly seventy years. *The Plowman Sings* aims to restore Sigmund to his rightful status as one of the most important and versatile players in the Regionalist movement.

Sigmund by Profession

Like Pulitzer Prize-winning poet Wallace Stevens, who turned down a faculty position at Harvard in order to remain vice president of The Hartford Accident and Indemnity Company, Jay G. Sigmund merged and blurred his vocation (insurance) and his avocation (writing). Insurance for Sigmund was both a means *and* an end: it allowed him to stay home, to remain in touch with the sublimities and the vulnerabilities of the people he represented. In fact, when Sigmund's Cedar Rapids Life Insurance Company merged with the Mutual of Omaha, Sigmund faced a Faustian bargain similar to Wallace Stevens's—move to Omaha at the behest of the company and continue on as vice president of a vastly expanded operation, or stay in his beloved Wapsipinicon Valley and look elsewhere for a job. Sigmund turned down the promotion and the paycheck, choosing to become, along with his son, James, an insurance operator with Twin Cities-based Minnesota Mutual Life, now Securian Financial. Then as now, Sigmund's successful career as a poet, fiction writer, and playwright is best considered alongside his "day job." Insurance, after all, was Sigmund's bread and butter, his window to the people of Iowa and the larger Midwest, with whose virtues and vices he was as well acquainted as a family doctor—a reoccurring character type in Sigmund's oeuvre, not coincidentally.

From the beginning, Jay Sigmund was a giver, a man who cheered the work of his disciples more than he did his own. His most famous young protégé was the poet and pioneer of the Iowa Writers' Workshop, Paul Engle, who neighbored and paperboyed for Sigmund in Cedar Rapids, Iowa. In his essay "Jay G. Sigmund as a Neighbor," published in Ed Ferreter's thesis "Grant Wood Meets Jay G. Sigmund," Engle recalls how Sigmund loaned him books, first by Longfellow and later by Edgar Lee Masters, William Carlos Williams, and "a husky man in Chicago writing about steel mills, corn, city streets, [and] laborers"—Carl Sandburg. Sigmund, whose work draws from Masters, Williams, and Sandburg, taught Engle that "nothing touched by the human hand or seen by human eyes, or used for work, or smelled or tasted, or spoken was unsuitable material for a poem." This same lesson formed the key plank in the platform of both the American Realists and Regionalists.

When later Sigmund moved with his wife to a new home in Cedar Rapids, fate dictated that their new address would once more fall within young Paul Engle's paper route. By this time, the great books independent study course Sigmund had been offering his young charge evolved to include translations of Arthur Rimbaud and Charles Baudelaire, poets who, while they eschewed Sigmund's plain style and palatability in favor of surrealism and sometimes willful obscurity, nonetheless evidenced Sigmund's belief in poetry's darker notes. When Engle later graduated from paperboy to pharmacy clerk, he recalled how Sigmund and his wife, Louise, would walk all the way from the edge of town to sit in Art Clark's drugstore where Engle worked. There, Engle reports, Clark ordered European literary magazines he knew would never sell simply to please Sigmund and to keep him coming back. Later, when Engle became an established poet in his own right, he would call on Sigmund at his insurance company, and Sigmund, predictably, would reveal a recent poem he had written, a guilty pleasure. "I always wondered," Engle mused, "how he divided his time between insurance papers and poetry texts."

Just how Sigmund divvyed up his professional attention remains a mystery, though the few who have written at length on Sigmund, including some who knew him, offer valuable insight. Ferreter describes Sigmund as "an excellent insurance salesman," a "mature person with an outgoing personality" whose interest in people came naturally. Engle, who introduces the only previously published, full-length anthology of Sigmund's works, *Select Poetry and Prose* (Prairie Press, 1939), captures the primacy of Sigmund's insurance work perfectly, writing, "He dwelt, as the American artist rightly should, in the very midst of the life around him, concerned with the affairs of his own city, involved with insurance, aware of the real contour of daily living in this place and time. He could not, as with so many of his contemporaries, ridicule our business civilization as wholly sterile and stupid. He knew it too intimately, being himself of it."

Sigmund reveals much of his double life as a successful insurance man and decorated creative writer in his all but forgotten one-act comedy *Vine Leaves*, which he coauthored, as he did nearly all his drama, with the University of North Carolina's Betty Smith. *Vine Leaves* tells the story of young Burt Judson, an "expert real estate salesman and poet," whose forthcoming poem in a literary magazine "outs" him as a versifier. While Sigmund and Smith take dramatic license, the play's autobiographical notes ring true. The president of the company, Mr. Leeper, tells his young employee, "Businessmen just don't write poetry." Indignant, Burt asks his boss why he isn't allowed to versify on his day off. If the competition discovered Burt's dirty secret, Mr. Leeper replies, his company would become "the laughing stock of the town."

And yet in Sigmund's dramatic art, as in his life, the relationship between poetry and business ultimately proved comedic in the literary sense of "happy endings." As the action in *Vine Leaves* reaches its climax, Mr. Leeper's real estate rivals enlist a poet to drum up demand for their new subdivision. Ironically, Burt Judson's poetic gift turns him from goat to hero when he crafts, at his bosses' behest, an extemporaneous poem that rivals the competition's and earns him the vice presidency of the firm—the exact position Sigmund held in real life. While Sigmund clearly did not trumpet his poetic inclinations to his bosses at the Cedar Rapids Life Insurance Company and later at Minnesota Mutual Life, evidence suggests he did not, either, try to hide his successful pastime, as insurance industry newsletters late in the author's life reference his literary reputation.

Similarly "scooping" the rare, virtuoso talent in their midst, the *Cedar Rapids Gazette* published an article in the mid 1930s about its native son under the title "Iowa Insurance Man Writes More Short Stories." Arriving on doorsteps across the city and state, the article featured a photo of Sigmund at his desk captioned "Looks more like his insurance side." In reviewing Sigmund's latest short story collection, *The Least of These*, writer Laurence Fairall wondered aloud "how many thousands of business men, school teachers, clerks, have said to themselves or to their friends, 'If I just had the time I could write short stories like that.' And how many disillusioned writers have told themselves 'I could have made plenty if I had gone into business.'" After inventorying Sigmund's various corporate bona fides—secretary of "Iowa's greatest insurance companies, a trainer of insurance salesmen, an executive . . . a go-getter," Fairall, juxtaposed the bustle of Sigmund's business days to the author's lonesomeness-infused fiction. Sigmund, he concluded, must be the Dr. Jekyll and Mr. Hyde of "Midwestern business and letters." Other reviewers, including Roland A. White, recast the apparent professional conundrum as a question of allegiance. In his column "Iowans in Ink: News and Reviews of Literary Iowans," Roland speculated, "The leftward-minded may think they find a comrade in Jay Sigmund at first, and wonder how it comes that he is vice president of an insurance company. The desperate situation of his tenant farmer friends is told so unsparingly, the crushing plight bared so sympathetically." Closer examination, though, White argued, showed that Sigmund was not the bleeding heart his fiction might at first suggest, but a careful witness to how "marginal land and the whims of nature" deepened the hard poverty of the author's native Wapsie Valley. Sigmund's villains, White reported, were not "straight-out capitalists," as would be the case if Sigmund were a closet leftist, but rather hucksters, peddlers, and charlatans. A February 24, 1924 review in the *New York Times* likewise singled out Sigmund's selflessness, noting, "What troubles the poet is not weeds in his maize and rye, but the inequalities of life—the desperate, bitter struggle of the underprivileged."

Others, including Cedar Rapids attorney Raymond Klass, divined some deeper logic in the businessman/author, Jekyll/Hyde dichotomy. Klass's musings, published in the *Cedar Rapids Republican* after that paper began running a once-per-week Sigmund short story, began with this simple premise: "No one sees all sides of human nature as the insurance salesman." The insurance man, Klass observed, "has seen a man insure his $400 automobile against fire and theft, the car which could be replaced, and then refuse to insure his own life in favor of wife and children. . . . He has seen a farmer insure his hogs for his own benefit and then refuse to insure his wife and babies. He has been frowned upon by the wife in taking the application and later met with the tears of gratitude as he brought in the amount of the policy in favor of the beneficiary. . . . In other words, Jay G. Sigmund has seen the human side of human nature."

Puzzling though it may have been, Sigmund shared his jack-of-all-trades, mixed professional inheritance with several of the great Modernists: William Carlos Williams made his living as a pediatrician; T. S. Eliot worked as a banker; and, of course, Wallace Stevens earned his paycheck as an insurance executive. More recently, in lamenting the loss of working poets like Sigmund, former U.S. Poet Laureate Ted Kooser, himself a retired vice president of the Lincoln (Nebraska) Benefit Life insurance company, wrote in the anthology *Black Earth and Ivory Tower*, "Until creative writers can no longer find work at universities and, to support themselves, have to farm or work in factories or sell shoes, most of our poetry and fiction will carry, as the poet Bob Phillips puts it, the odor of the lamp." Kooser writes in praise of what avocational poets Williams, Eliot, Stevens, and Sigmund offered—the social capital and local economies made possible when writers draw their material sustenance from the very place they draw their writerly "material." Concluding his essay "Jay G. Sigmund as a Neighbor," Engle likewise appreciates Sigmund's wholehearted presence in his community, writing, "Not every street should have its own poet, but surely every city should. Jay was there as a living presence of poetry for me. Every young kid wanting to write should be so lucky."

Jay Sigmund and Grant Wood

While the younger Paul Engle would become Jay Sigmund's greatest, champion, Sigmund's influence, literary and artistic, among his age peers proved still more pronounced. Famously, Sigmund is credited with launching his friend and fellow Cedar Rapids resident Grant Wood on the path to artistic stardom, a subject taken up at length in Edward Ferreter's "Grant Wood Meets Jay G. Sigmund." Ferreter, characterizing the Sigmund-Wood relationship as "a unique example of artistic symbiosis," nonetheless spills a good deal of ink on the differences between the two Iowa visionaries. While both were farm-born artists who grew up near the Wapsipinicon River (Wood in Anamosa, Iowa; Sigmund in nearby Waubeek), Wood studied art in Chicago, Minneapolis, and Paris, and later taught at the University of Iowa, while Sigmund, an autodidact, finished his formal schooling with the tenth grade. Wood, an early artistic bloomer who traveled to Europe multiple times in his younger days and delayed marriage, contrasted dramatically with Sigmund, who, Ferreter notes, married early and never made it beyond Chicago. Sigmund's reputation for business—Carl Sandburg once described him in the *Chicago Daily News* as a "big insurance man of Cedar Rapids"—afforded him, his wife, and their three children a summer home in Sigmund's hometown of Waubeek. Grant Wood, by contrast, cobbled together teaching jobs and commissions and, early on, led the life of the "starving artist."

These very differences fueled a friendship that compares favorably with the most electric, most productive artistic partnerships of the time—comparable in historical significance to the provocative, often fraught relationships between Ezra Pound and T. S. Eliot, for example, or Sherwood Anderson and Ernest Hemingway. In each of these partnerships, one man's career blossomed disproportionately. In the Sigmund-Wood relationship, Sigmund sacrificed some of the energies that might have been reserved for his own work to aid Wood's cause. The two developed a close, if not pungent, association, according to Ferreter, via the Grant Wood Garlic Club, a downtown Cedar Rapids lunch group consisting of Grant Wood, Marvin Cone, MacKinlay Kantor, Don Defore, and Fran Alison. A young, not yet world-famous Grant Wood held court, tossing a communal salad while the members supplied the vinegar and oil. In a variant of "can't-stand-the-heat-get-out-of-the-kitchen," Garlic Clubbers tested prospective members with the group's strong odors, intellectual and otherwise.

Fortunately for the art world, Grant Wood suffered well, and learned from, the aesthetic provocations and interrogations Sigmund directed his way. Many historians now credit Sigmund with turning Grant Wood's attentions back to Iowa. Jim Sigmund, Jay's son, told Ferreter of a time when Wood had come to visit the Sigmunds at their summer home in Waubeek, on which occasion he overheard his father take Wood to task for being a "copycat" of the French when he could be painting the "beauties of Iowa." Sigmund, forever the instigator, illustrated native splendor by pointing down his Waubeek street to where two painted quilts hung. Those very quilts from the summer of 1928, Ferreter reports, became the subject of Grant Wood's early impressionistic painting, "Quilts."

A February 16, 1969 article in the *Cedar Rapids Gazette* confirms Jim Sigmund's retelling. The article, citing the then-opening of a Grant Wood retrospective at the Cedar Rapids Museum of Art, recollects an earlier Wood exhibit, this one at the Cedar Rapids Public Library in the 1920s and featuring Wood's Parisian street scenes. While the show ran, one of Sigmund's poems, entitled "Grant Wood" and featuring a young man dreaming on the plains, appeared in the *Gazette* and caught Wood's eye. The *Gazette* reported that Wood was so impressed with the idea of the poem that it "gave him an idea" to paint "Iowa scenes." "There followed," the newspaper concluded, "a whole series of paintings which made Grant Wood famous and regional art a national vogue."

In 1926, Wood and Sigmund had only begun to cross paths, artistically and literally. Always, the two men shared stomping grounds. Stone City, Iowa, the model for what many art critics consider Wood's first major landscape painting and the site of Wood's renowned Stone City Art Colony, Sigmund likewise held sacred. The village itself, soon to be made famous, lies roughly equidistant between Sigmund's Waubeek and Grant Wood's Anamosa. When Wood and fellow painter and teacher Marvin Cone opened the art colony 1932 and 1933, it served as a logical meeting point for Wood, Sigmund, Cone, Engle, and others in the Regionalist avant-garde. Ferreter relays how Sigmund would serve as master of ceremonies for the Sunday afternoon fundraising performances—ten cents per head—put on by the art colony's teachers and students. The author would then read his poetry as part of the night's entertainments and would otherwise serve as a fly on the wall during the sometimes comical, occasionally raucous events. Sigmund's one-act play *Folk Stuff*, coauthored with Betty Smith and reprinted for the first time in this anthology, suggests the high spiritedness of the Stone City Art Colony in its heyday and, moreover, some of the pretensions inherent in the Regionalist movement itself.

In many instances, the shared lives of the two Iowa luminaries passed directly into art. A case in point is Wood's dramatic painting "Death on Ridge Road," a canvas he undertook after visiting the site of a real-life automobile accident suffered by Sigmund and his wife after a Sunday art colony performance. Louise broke several ribs and doctors were forced to amputate the index finger of Sigmund's right hand, a hand he would later adapt for use in his work as a sculptor and woodcarver. In fact, Sigmund the artist earns a stand-alone entry in Zenobia B. Ness and Louise Orwig's *Iowa Artists of the First 100 Years* as a "Sculptor and Wood Carver" in his own right. Utterly self-taught in art as in writing, Sigmund's sculpture "Judas" delighted visitors at the All Iowa Exhibit in January 1937, while his wood carvings decorated Cedar Rapids's Grace Church.

While Sigmund's crash-up directly inspired Grant Wood's "Death on Ridge Road," elsewhere the Sigmund-Wood cross-pollination shows up in more subtle, less literal ways. Wood's painting "Spring in Town" takes as its setting, according to Ferreter, Sigmund's backyard in Waubeek. Moreover, while Wood's plan to paint a formal portrait of his good friend was thwarted by Sigmund's untimely death in 1937, Wood did, Ferreter notes, use Sigmund as a model for the man peering over his (Wood's) shoulder in "Return from Bohemia." Beyond these cameos on canvas, subject matter for Sigmund's poetry and Wood's paintings ran parallel. Sigmund's poem "Death Rides a Rubber Shod Horse," in which a car becomes a "devil-horse of steel and brass," may be considered a de facto prose companion piece to Wood's "Death on the Ridge Road." Similarly, Sigmund's "Stone City" poem matches up well with Wood's "Stone City" canvas, and so on throughout the work of both Regionalist visionaries.

Beyond Grant Wood, Jay Sigmund and Friends

Though he remained close to home, relishing the role of a "provincial" writer, Jay G. Sigmund maintained literary ties both wide and deep. Beyond his mail-only collaboration with playwriting partner Betty Smith, which produced one-acts for top companies such as Samuel French and The Dramatic Publishing Company, Sigmund enjoyed entertaining literary luminaries in person. Guests at the Sigmund summer home in Waubeek included, according to Ferreter, John T. Frederick and Carl Sandburg, who Sigmund met at Cornell College in Mount Vernon, Iowa. In turn, Sandburg introduced Sigmund to the members of the Chicago Renaissance, a group of literati that included Sinclair Lewis, H. L. Mencken, Sherwood Anderson, and, on occasion, Gertrude Stein. Ferreter reports that Sigmund made the trip to Chicago as often as he could, usually riding the train to Union Station every few months. With more far-flung kindred souls, especially Ilya Tolstoy, Robinson Jeffers, Edmund Blunden, and Charles Finger, Sigmund sustained warm relations by pen and ink.

Among Sigmund's high-profile associations, his relationship with Sherwood Anderson stands out as the most uncanny. After Anderson, author of the classic *Winesburg, Ohio*, left Chicago to became the editor of the *Smythe County News* and the *Marion Democrat* in Marion, Virginia, he urged Sigmund to submit poems to his newspapers. Anderson's third wife, Elizabeth, recounts in *Miss Elizabeth: A Memoir* how Anderson "invented" several of his alleged newspaper reporters and contributors, including a "Mrs. Homing Pigeon," a "Colonel Star Dust," and "Al Jackson," a correspondent from the New Orleans swamps. In itself, Anderson's use of fictional personas is relatively common. But, almost as an afterthought, Mrs. Anderson remarks, "Almost all of the poetry in the paper was written by Sherwood under the name Jay G. Sigmund." While Sigmund biographer Edward Ferreter hastens to add that "Sherwood Anderson was not a plagiarist in the ordinary sense," he does admit that Anderson "stole" Sigmund's name and "led everyone to believe that the name Jay Sigmund was his [Anderson's] pseudonym." The ruse, according to Ferreter, was sufficiently seamless to fool both Elizabeth Anderson and literary critic Stuart Chase, who, reviewing Anderson's volume of collected material from the newspapers, *Hello Towns*, enthused, "There was one poem 'Land Locked Sailor' which brought me near to genuine tears. It was written by a Jay G. Sigmund, obviously a pseudonym." While Ferreter exonerates Anderson in claiming, "Anderson did not plagiarize Jay Sigmund's poetry," contemporary examples of "flattery" plagiarism, such as the one suffered by Iowa poet Neal Bowers and retold in Bowers's *Words for the Taking: The Hunt for a Plagiarist* suggest that Sigmund, had he been fully aware of Anderson's duplicity, might indeed have felt aggrieved.

As suggested by Chase's effusive praise for "Land Locked Sailor," Sigmund's poetry earned national acclaim, In addition to positive, published reviews by Carl Sandburg and unpublished letters of praise from the likes of Ilya

Tolstoy, H. L. Mencken, Robinson Jeffers, and Edmund Blunden, Lew Sarett, professor at Northwestern University, advisory editor of *Poetry* magazine, and a renowned nature poet, praised "the sincerity and the smell of the earth" in Sigmund's poetry. Writing for the *Saturday Review of Literature* in February 1931, William Rose Benét commented, "Mr. Sigmund's honesty is something, and his stories are really indigenous." In the June 30, 1929 *Des Moines Register*, the column "Iowa Writers" noted, "There is no Iowa writer about whom more inquiries come in than Jay G. Sigmund of Cedar Rapids; probably he himself would be surprised to know how many Iowa clubs have made him the object of carefully prepared papers." The *Register* feature went on to list published praise for Sigmund, including an endorsement by George Russell (A.E.) who, the column claimed, "has enthusiastically praised his [Sigmund's] verse and published it," adding that critic Keith Preston had written, "'He [Sigmund] does the kind of stuff that is hailed as genius in Scandinavian or Russian realists and ignored for the most part in our own national writers.'" The *Register* concluded, "One could go on quoting enthusiastic comments from people like Robinson Jeffers, William Ellery Leonard, George Sterling, Julia Peterkin, H. L. Mencken, Harriet Monroe, Edmund Blunden, and many others. It is evident that Mr. Sigmund has won the admiration and respect of critics whose approval is coveted by any contemporary creative writers."

Indeed, Sigmund's Midwest-centric work merited praise from reviewers across the globe. Ilya Tolstoy hailed Sigmund as "an American Chekhov and Maupassant." Iowa readers, meanwhile, were reminded of Sigmund's growing international reputation in 1931 when the *Cedar Rapids Gazette* reprinted portions of a review of Sigmund's collection *The Ridge Road* as it had appeared in a literary magazine from England, *Poetry and the Play*. "It is regrettable," the *Gazette* quoted an unnamed English reviewer as saying, "that there are no English editions of Mr. Sigmund's books . . . for there are many American writers who are known here and whose claims are of a lower kind." Of the same book, critic Gene Morgan wrote, "*The Ridge Road* goes further to establish his [Sigmund's] unique position as bard and interpreter of Corn Belt folks."

In 1927's *Wapsipinicon Tales* Sigmund tried his hand at fiction and met with almost instant success. In his prefatory essay to the *Wapsipinicon* story cycle, Newberry Prize-winning fiction writer Charles J. Finger wrote, "Here comes my friend, Jay G. Sigmund, offering nothing but the romance of the commonplace, yet telling a tale as breathlessly interesting as if he had written of two doughty knights spilling each other's blood." Finger's introduction, and Sigmund's growing literary reputation, prompted reviews of *Wapsipinicon Tales* across the Midwest and Great Plains. Writing for the July 5, 1927 *Emporia* (Kansas) *Gazette*, one reviewer, assigned the initials L. R. C., echoed Finger's praise for the "commonplace subjects" about which Sigmund wrote with an empathy which "the average writer never would see, much less write about." Noting that many of the stories in the book appeared in "the best magazines in the country," the reviewer concluded, "And above all, the stories are interesting . . . These stories represent people, things, customs. They were not written merely to amuse the great throng of readers who seek sensation and thrill in their books. Yet there is a thrill in Sigmund's stories, a thrill born of reality which is startling."

In *Wapsipinicon Tales*, Jay Sigmund created a particular, based-on-real-life landscape of "little Wapsipinicon town[s]" similar to the Lake Woebegone environs Garrison Keillor would create a half century later. But while Keillor chose easy humor and warm parable to endear the residents of Lake Woebegone to a national audience, Sigmund's fiction takes on the documentary quality of good, hard-hitting journalism. The method met with mixed success and much comment in the national and regional press. In his *All's Well* literary magazine, Charles Finger lionized his friend's courage in writing material for which, "as all the world knows, there is no market . . . in the magazines of today when the cry is all for unconvincing romanticism, success and sex tales, and stories of impossible adventure—but that matters no more to Sigmund than it mattered to Millet that no dealer wanted his pictures." For others, Sigmund's unflinching realism had itself become an exaggeration, as William Rose Benét claimed in his May 16, 1931 review in *The Saturday Review of Literature*. While praising Sigmund for his honesty, Benét insisted, "Mr. Sigmund deals in tragic materials, but it takes a [Sherwood] Anderson to bring out the essentials of tragedy among the dwellers in a Winesburg—or a Wapsipinicon Valley."

In *A Literary History of Iowa* (1972), Clarence A. Andrews shared Benét's ambivalent view. Calling Sigmund's portrayals in *Wapsipinicon Tales* and elsewhere "Perhaps the dreariest pictures of farm life," Andrews suggested that Sigmund's work suffered from a trend then affecting many of the writers publishing in John T. Frederick's Iowa-based national journal, *The Midland*. Andrews quotes Phil Stong's reminiscence in *Hawkeyes* at length: "during my college years, 1915-1919, all of us little farmhands were trying to make *The Midland*. The method was to summon up memories of the most miserable and feckless family we had ever heard of around the home town, adorn them with some tragic graces and see that one or all of the outfit 1) went crazy 2) murdered the others 3) committed suicide, incest, or arson before the end of the story. It was Eugene O'Neill gone made in the pigpens." Still, the pointed though good-humored critique of what might be called "The Midland method" is not as germane to Sigmund, who did not attend college and purposefully eschewed allegiance to any "school" of writing.

To his credit, Andrews, while criticizing Sigmund's work for its sometimes darkness, wrote, "A few Iowa poets have gained distinction for their poetry about the farm. One is Jay Sigmund; another is Paul Engle, whose early ventures in the writing of poetry were encouraged by Sigmund." John T. Frederick, who published many of Sigmund's works in *The Midland*, captured his friend's greatness, inclusive of his comedic and tragic pieces, in an essay entitled "The New Realism" from the March 1951 issue of the *Palimpsest*, wherein he wrote, "Sigmund had a keen eye for the eccentric, the comic, and a warm sense of humor. He had also a deep sense of the tragic reality which often underlies a surface seemingly dull and prosaic." Considering Sigmund's short fiction alongside his poetry, Frederick closed, "His [Sigmund's] interpretation of Iowa farm people... has been surpassed only by the work of James Hearst."

In 1937 Sigmund's career as a popular writer peaked. From January to October of that year, the *Chicago Tribune* ran a serial Sigmund poem in its "A Line O' Type or Two" column, exposing tens of thousands of Chicagoans each week to the agrarian philosophies of an Iowa poet. In the April 25 edition of that same year, the *Tribune* followed up with a lengthy article entitled "Iowa College Out with New Chapbooks" heralding Cornell College's publication of Sigmund's book of poems *Heron at Sunset*. Writer John Evans wrote of the collection: "His [Sigmund's] spontaneity raises his verse to the level of poetry. The vacuity of retirement, the surge of spring, the terror of the trapped, the depression of autumn, the futility of senility, the loneliness of winter, all these simple but poignant emotions are aroused in the reader, not by the artifice of cadence, but by the art of creation." In his introduction to the volume, Cornell College professor and series editor Clyde Tull, offered, "Mr. Sigmund's work is characterized by fine sincerity, a thoroughgoing sympathy for the small town and country folks he portrays so vividly in his stories and verse, and a quiet mastery of technique that attracts little attention to itself but gives pleasure to the discriminating."

On October 22, 1937, eager readers opened their *Chicago Tribune* to find a poem entitled "Jay G. Sigmund's Last Poem." The fine print below the verse read: "The poem above, 'Early Fall Evening,' was the last received by *The Line* from Mr. Sigmund, celebrated poet of Cedar Rapids, Iowa, whose career was ended by a hunting tragedy."

Three days later, on October 25th, *Tribune* readers wrote in with their eulogies, among them a short poem entitled "Lines to Jay G. Sigmund" that appeared in the space in "A Line O' Type or Two" ordinarily reserved for Sigmund. Its elegy is apt: "He sang of hills and fields and earthy things, / of furrowed rows all ready for the seed. / He wrote in cadence rich of harvest time." Lamenting the irony of the author's tragic death—"How very meet that Death should seek him out / There in those woods he loved so knowing well"—the verse concludes, "Farewell, rare singer of fine songs, / We'll miss your telling of a Winter's Tale."

Sigmund Passing

The official cause of the October 19, 1937 death was a "hunting accident" in which, as Clarence Andrews put it, "he [Sigmund] was accidentally wounded by a blast from his own shotgun as he hunted near his home by the river." In a prefatory note to the posthumous Sigmund tribute collection, *Select Poetry and Prose*, Paul Engle remembered: "Marvin Cone drove out to Stone City October 20, 1937, and told me of Jay Sigmund's death. It was a dark day, rain coming up in flurries. I was chopping wood. We stood and looked down at the Wapsie, flowing with an autumn brown. I had been walking along it the day before, at the same hour when Jay was lying in the field calling for help in the empty air." Upon hearing Cone's news, Engle could think of nothing better to do with his sadness than to write an elegy, which he titled "Jay G. Sigmund," and which concludes, "We knew him too, we were his friends / From the farming country around / The Wapsie land where he lived and worked / We know the feel of that ground // We will die different men because / We knew him face to face. / Let us bury him now with his weather and his crops, / And say—He belongs to this place."

The *Cedar Rapids Gazette*, Sigmund's hometown newspaper and a longtime supporter of his work, broke the news to the city under the headline "Cedar Rapids Poet Is Shot While Hunting; Leg Amputation Fails to Save Life of Businessman and Writer." The October 20, 1937 obituary opened, "Jay G. Sigmund, Cedar Rapids poet, and one of the Midwest's most prominent writers and lecturers on literature, died in a local hospital at 9:10 P.M. Tuesday following amputation of his left leg after a hunting accident near his summer home in Waubeek Tuesday afternoon." The article detailed how the 51-year-old Sigmund had lost his footing while following a wounded rabbit in the pastures near his summer home and had accidentally discharged his shotgun into his leg below the knee.

The *Gazette* covered Sigmund's well-attended funeral under the headline "Extols Sigmund's Life and Writings . . . Father Campbell Speaking at Funeral Service Refers to Businessman-Poet as Complete Personality." Father Campbell, emphasizing Sigmund's well-rounded character, reminded mourners that "a saint is a whole person—a complete personality, so I place him [Sigmund] with the saints." Indeed, the diversity of the estimated 500 attendees, reported as a mix of "members of the local insurance agents association . . . as well as representatives of the various art, literary, and civic groups to which he [Sigmund] belonged" testified to the author's outreach. Father Campbell, the article reported, said he "hoped the farmers and townspeople of Waubeek . . . would raise a monument to the memory of the man who lived among them, wrote among them."

Appropriately, given that Sigmund had left his home on the fatal day to hunt mushrooms, those speaking at the funeral focused on his enduring legacy as a naturalist-poet. Among those offering eulogies, Sigmund's neighbor John Wagor remembered fondly Sigmund's love of nature. Fred Poyneer called Sigmund a "student of the outdoors" and a man who "knew the spirit as well as the technical side of nature." Perry Buxton of the *Wheatland Gazette* celebrated Sigmund's ability to "take the smoke of autumn or the flight of a hawk and interpret it for us." Dr. H. M. Gage, president of Cedar Rapids's Coe College, urged grievers not to focus on the words coming from rostrum but on themselves. "This is what Jay would have wanted," Gage said, looking out over the diverse crowd. "Just folks with all their folkishness."

While no statues were erected in Sigmund's honor, friends created a memorial and later a park in Sigmund's hometown of Waubeek. The memorial, a bronze tablet set in rough stone, reads, "To Jay G. Sigmund who by the goodness of his living and the beauty of his writing gave back to the people of the

Wapsie Valley that joy they had given him." In Cedar Rapids, Coe College marked the poet's passing by publishing a limited-edition collection entitled *The Hawk That Haunts the Sky*. "In tribute to Mr. Sigmund's interest in young writers and his friendship for the Writer's Club," the dedication to the in-memoriam volume read, "we here reprint several of his favorite poems."

While tributes rolled in from newspaper reporters, college presidents, and literary greats on the occasion of Sigmund's death, an article from the mid 1920s, printed in response to the publication by the *Cedar Rapids Republican* of Sigmund's serial short stories, typifies the warm feelings for him held by everyday readers. The collection of reader opinions, entitled "Local Folk Appreciate Sigmund's Short Story," led with the following testimony: "'He is ours,' says Wilmer C. Jones, local railway mailclerk, in commenting upon Jay G. Sigmund, known now as the 'poet of the Wapsipinicon,' but who, it seems, will soon earn the title of 'Washington Irving of Iowa.'" The article continues, "It is true that he [Sigmund] belongs to a nationwide following of literary critics. Nevertheless, the folk of Cedar Rapids are going to be the ones to judge his latest literary efforts." The article next elicits reactions from a cross section of Sigmund's hometown peers—railway clerks, bookstore managers, city commissioners, authors, attorneys, school superintendents, college professors, and pastors. Mrs. Teeter, head of the book department at Morris Sanford stores, commented, "I believe it is going to be possible for Mr. Sigmund to express in these stories even better than in his poetry, the great fund of material that he has accumulated as he has observed folks—real Iowa folks."

The Sigmund Legacy

Jay Sigmund continues to inspire unusual loyalty among the few who keep his legacy alive. In the late 1980s, Edward Ferreter, a 30-year veteran of the postal service in Sigmund's native Wapsie Valley, completed a short Master's thesis on Sigmund in addition to publishing a chapbook-length work of photos and accompanying Sigmund poems in an informal volume titled "Jay Sigmund's Wapsipinicon Valley" in the Central City, Iowa newsletter. Still, despite such Sigmund stalwarts, the latter-day resurrection of his work that Charles Finger dared hope for has not happened, or at least not as Finger originally envisioned. Writing in his literary magazine *All's Well* shortly after the publication of Sigmund's *Least of These* in 1935, Finger predicted, "Some day, when historians of the future cast about in newspapers and magazines for material to enable them to reconstruct ways of life in the Middle West, and are disappointed, some one may exhume Sigmund's books from among my collection, and great will be the joy of the discoverer." While Finger's endorsement is genuine, his comments suggest a fledging theory for why Jay G. Sigmund is not better remembered. Perhaps Sigmund's status as an interpreter and documentarian of his people, a cultural anthropologist of a sort, has caused readers to overlook the literary merit of his writings. An equally plausible factor may be Sigmund's premature death at age 51, truncating what would doubtless have been a prolific retirement. Certainly, Sigmund's refusal to leave home, coupled with his insistence on earning a workaday living, has disadvantaged his reputation by comparison with midwestern literary peers: principally Fitzgerald, Hemingway, Sandburg, and Anderson. Arguably, Sigmund's scruples prevented him from attracting still greater notice in the Jazz Age—lacking, as he was, the mental illness, the alcoholism, and the multiple marriages mined for material by his more infamous colleagues. In the end, maybe the place he loved, a Wapsie Valley of undersized hill farms and tenant plowmen poor by comparison with the rest of Iowa, thwarted stardom from the start. Or maybe Jay Sigmund, who began writing seriously at age 36, came along just a little too late, traveling in the footsteps of Hamlin Garland, Sherwood Anderson, and Edgar Lee Masters, who had previously played many of the same notes. Of course, those remotely familiar with Sigmund should at least consider an alternate theory, one radical in its simplicity: Jay Sigmund did not covet fame.

In any case, Sigmund's star burned especially brightly from 1927 to his death in 1937, a decade in which he lived at the heart of the Regionalist movement, mentored the next generation of Iowa writers, launched Grant Wood, and brought the literary attentions of the nation back to Iowa. In 1930, after Boston editor Edward J. O'Brien listed an unbelievable six Sigmund short stories among "The Best Short Stories of 1930," headlines such as this one appeared in the *Des Moines Register*: "Iowa City Now U.S. Literary Center, Suggests E. J. O'Brien, Noted Critic." The banner headline was accompanied by photos of seven of Iowa's top writers, Jay G. Sigmund among them, and a map of the United States showing a line drawn directly from Boston, through New York City, and terminating in Eastern Iowa. The sudden success of midwestern small-town and farm-born writers prompted much speculation in the Eastern press, and much glee in places like Des Moines, where Iowa native Thomas W. Duncan published an article entitled "To the Hills, Men, the Dam's Busted" in which he exhorted 1930s writers, "To the hills! To the prairies! Any place where land is uncrowded and where the doubtful virtues of concrete highways are unknown." Writing that a "sense of the pastoral has always been in great poetry," Duncan declared, "Jim Hearst is the wisest poet in Iowa. He is living on the soil. Jay Sigmund is wise. He's writing about the soil." In 1935, Roland A. White, reviewing Sigmund's *The Least of These* and *Burroak and Sumac* in his "Iowans in Ink: News and Reviews of Literary Iowans" column, imagined the bracing effect Sigmund's work would have on "sophisticates in New York" who would have their "vanity rubbed the right way by the hick atmosphere of [Sigmund's] Ontarns, a village in the Wapsipinicon region." "This book," White insisted, "is not for escapists or time whilers." If sophisticates needed a daily dose of literary condescension, they would not find it in Sigmund, who, White wrote, writes "like a good neighbor."

In the end, Sigmund's most valuable legacy resides among the people who knew him best, his neighbors. Of these, Paul Engle best articulates his mentor's trailblazing. Engle writes, "He was what ideally a poet should always be, not a person removed from the world, set apart from its ordinary life, but a man dwelling among men, aware of the urgency in their daily affairs. He was a neighbor before he was a writer, a human being before he was an artist." Engle continues, "Here to me is the most magnificent aspect of Jay Sigmund, that he helped to make a city and a country not merely good places to raise a family, but to write a poem or paint a picture. He made art at home in a little area of the earth. This is a great destiny for any man." Through the radical act of staying home to make a sparsely populated agricultural state a worldwide literary center, Jay Sigmund proved that deep roots were not just possible in the world of letters but indispensable.

In 1934, just a year before Jay G. Sigmund's most productive year as a writer and only three years before his tragic death, Wendell Berry, Sigmund's natural heir, was born in rural Henry County, Kentucky. Though, unlike Sigmund, Wendell Berry would attend college and would spend his adult life teaching in universities, Berry effectively expressed to subsequent generations what Sigmund had known all along. In his quintessential essay of homecoming, "A Native Hill," Berry speaks to the primacy of his home place, Port Royal, Kentucky, writing, "When I have thought of the welfare of the earth, the problems of health and preservation, the care of its life, I have had this place before me, the part representing the whole more vividly and accurately, making clearer and more pressing demands, than any *idea* of the whole. When I have thought of kindness or cruelty, weariness or exuberance, devotion or betrayal, carelessness or care, doggedness or awkwardness or grace, I have had in my mind's eye the men and women of this place, their faces and gestures and movements."

As the valley of the Kentucky River was to Wendell Berry, the Wapsie Valley was to Jay Sigmund. As early as *Pinions* in 1923, Sigmund distinguished himself as a poet of the *environment*, not just of nature, a fact well noted in the first-ever *New York Times* review of his work, which read, in part: "It is evident that the author is familiar with the woodland and the marshes, with the nighthawk and the plover and the purple martin, with the toad and the muskrat and the garden snail. . . . It is poetry full of sights and sounds, the smells and colors of the field and the woodland. There are in it that sense of freshness and surprise, that breath of field folk and orchard trees that can only be given back in poetry by one who has learned their names and all their secrets."

Often reviewed and written about during his lifetime, Sigmund was seldom interviewed. Perhaps he considered conducting an interview an unwarranted intrusion on his business day; more likely he wanted his work to speak for itself. But appended to a *Des Moines Register* June 30, 1929 feature on Sigmund is a section wherein the editors of the "Iowa Writers" column print Sigmund's mailed-in reply to their query about his favorite poem. Sigmund wrote that his own poem of greatest literary merit was probably "River Road Wedlock." But he enclosed as his true favorite the short poem "Morning Mists on the Wapsipinicon," with the following note, "If you reprint this I hope it will be done with the understanding that as a poem I don't consider it much, but I like it because it interprets a good mood that often comes to me when I wander along my beloved

Wapsipinicon River."

The first two stanzas of "Morning Mists" distill the spirit of the man perfectly, locating in the selfsame Iowa soil both ecstatic, ritual openings and final, funereal curtain calls:

>Evening brought by whippoorwills
>Morning ushered in by thrushes
>Midnight brooding on my hills—
>Soft frog croonings in my rushes.
>
>These few things I'll always keep
>Always hold and ever cherish—
>Man is sure of loam-locked sleep
>Then his fragile dreams must perish.

I.
Fiction

The Foot Hoe

All through the sweltering June afternoon, fifteen-year-old Roger Blake had plodded behind his walking cornplow, and the dust kept blowing up from the shovels to sting and choke.

It is a long afternoon when one must follow down the rows and see the great Mississippi roll slowly by at the foot of the knoll, where you are held by the confines of its barbed wire fences, for the great river seems to be saying *Come, I'm going to the ocean. You will never get anywhere if you merely walk back and forth on that cornfield hill behind those bony horses!*

Roger could have stood it all well enough, but for the smartweeds in the corn hills. It was almost maddening to think of the bullheads hungry for grasshoppers in the nearby bayou, and it brought misery to think of the heron roost up the river, where sets of green heron eggs lay, sea-green in twig nests waiting for someone to collect them, blow them, and have them ready to exchange with other collectors next fall. But the real physical pain, the acute biting ache, came from endless bending over corn hills to tear tough-rooted smartweeds from the loam.

The shovels of his plow he dared not hold too close for fear he would plow out the tender corn. "Be sure to get all the smartweed out of the hills," his practical-minded father had told him that morning. What did his father care for an aching back? Roger could see him over on the river bottom as he rode the mower around the field of alfalfa, and leveled a sickle's width of the emerald hay each round.

As he plodded along, stopping every now and then to bend over a hill of corn, the tired youth mused over his lot as many an older man has done. It seemed the irritating rounds of farm work were becoming more and more irksome. The year before Roger had not plowed corn. He was considered too young and had weeded onions instead. His father always raised an acre of this vegetable in a low spot of rich alluvial land along the Mississippi.

But this year he had been taken out of school to "harrow down stalks." Later he had ridden on a disc, and after planting time, he was put to dropping pumpkin seeds up and down the corn rows with a sharp stick which made a hole into which he placed four seeds, and then covered them with his foot.

Next came corn plowing and the smartweeds, muscle sting and choking dust, boiling sun and short nights, with his father pounding on his bedroom door just as the great red sun spilled its first rays on the river as it crawled over the hills on the Illinois side.

At last, when draughts from his stone water jug, which he had put under a wild cherry tree at the margin of the field, failed to refresh him longer, he lay down for a while under a great cottonwood. From where he lay he could see the alfalfa field and when his father stopped his mower for several minutes, Roger knew he was watching and wondering why the team was not making its rounds with the cornplow, so he arose and stretched his aching arms, and once again started across the field.

The smartweeds seemed to be getting thicker all the time! Nearly every hill now had a bunch of them. It seemed the aching in his back would grow unbearable.

At last he began trying a new plan. He would uproot the smartweeds with the toe of his shoe! The first trial or two was successful for the soil here was loose. What a relief it was on the muscles of his tired back.

But soon he struck a span of clay soil and the thrusts he made with his foot only bent the clumps of weeds down, and he had to stop the team and bend over and pull the tough weeds again. Now he noticed that even his wrist was growing lame and sore from the strain.

But suddenly a dream began taking shape in his brain. If one could only make a sort of iron blade and strap it to his toes and cut the smartweeds out without bending his back. He thought of such an instrument with a feeling of joy as he turned his team around at the end of the field. What a labor-saver! What a boon to weary farmers and farmers' sons especially!

The joy of discovery—of creative impulse—surged through him.

It could be made of sheet iron, he reasoned in his brain. It would be shaped to slide over the toe of the shoe, and a crescent-shaped knife would extend out from the shoe sole. The wearer could walk along between the handles of his plow, and when he came to a hill of corn which contained a clump of weeds, a skillful swing of the foot, and the weeds would be uprooted and the weary muscles saved unnecessary strain.

The more the youth thought of it, the more plausible the thing seemed. He had heard of inventors dreaming out things which were to revolutionize the world. He remembered in his school history the story of Robert Fulton and his steamboat, of Howe and his sewing machine, of Watts and his steam engine.

He tried to picture himself as a hero in the neighborhood, and he saw in his mind's eye the *Daleport Gazette* with great headlines announcing his invention: "Ord County farm boy invents great device," the paper might say. Then it would go on perhaps something like: "This fortunate young man has just received a patent, and a local plow manufacturing concern is taking the article over to make on a royalty."

Although it was only half past three o'clock when the idea came to Roger, the rest of the afternoon sped rapidly. It seemed only a few minutes until Roger saw his father stop at one end of the field and wave his hand at him—the signal that it was "quitting time."

Roger's step was light as he drove his team into the barnyard. He had been a little perplexed as how best to break the news of his great idea to his father, but, though he knew the gruffness of his father's nature made him always skeptical to anything new, it seemed to the youth that here was one thing that must surely arouse enthusiasm in his parent.

He watered his team at the tank. It seemed to him they were more thirsty than usual and drank more slowly.

On the way from the field he had tried to imagine the conversation with his father. He had even tired to imagine the surprised look on his father's face as he told him of the proposed invention which he had made up his mind would be called a "foot-hoe."

His father was tossing corn to a bunch of grunting hogs when he finished unharnessing his horses, so Roger, knowing the difficulty of trying to make himself heard under such circumstances, waited until his father came shuffling up the path from the hog pen.

The old man carried the basket at his side and his blue hickory shirt was soaked with sweat. He pulled at his scraggly grey mustache with one hand as he approached the barn door and gave a glance of surprise at Roger. Roger seldom stood around idle at chore time.

Roger immediately began to tell his father of his "foot-hoe."

He knew it would take all the enthusiasm at his command to convert his stolid sire. Elaborating as much as he could, he explained in detail the great idea which had come to him. He showed with well-chosen arguments, the disadvantages of having to stop so often to pull weeds from corn hills. He bent low to show his father the position one must assume to reach the weeds and he twisted his body and grimaced to show the strain on muscles as one tore the weeds from the soil. All the eloquence he could command he used. He showed the old farmer who stood beside him how the "foot-hoe" would be made, adjusted to the toe, and used.

His father stood and listened. There was no change in the expression on his face while Roger was talking, but at last the boy spent all the force of his argument and brought in the final clincher which had come into his mind on the way in from the field. His face flushed and his voice raised to a high pitch. "And Pa," he said with fervor, "if it turns out well, I'll help you pay off all you owe on the place!"

His father now spoke for the first time, and as he spoke he started away with a gesture of impatience:

"You're always thinkin' of some way to get out of work," he grumbled, "go throw down hay for the horses. It's late!"

Dubbing Season

Alva Whitfield walked down the clamshell bordered path, which led from his little white cottage, and as he passed the opening in the wall of wild cucumber draped fence, he stood for a moment and looked over the hazel brush toward the Wapsipinicon, where the August heat danced above the bluish ribbon of stream.

The yellow sand bar, which stuck out in the bayou like a frail finger, claimed his attention as a pair of green herons hovered above it. For a moment Alva's thoughts went back to the spring before, when he had shot five bald-pates on that same sand bar.

But since the hunting season had come the hatching season, and Alva had set more of his Warhorse game hens this year than ever before. The result was more stags than he had ever had on range in any one year.

Outside of his hunting and trapping, nothing interested the gaunt river road bachelor more than his flock of game fowls. Usually silent and shy, he became almost eloquent when explaining to a stranger about his birds. For hours, if the listener was patient enough, Alva would talk of different strains of fighting fowl, of various makes and styles of steel spurs, of training methods and feeding tricks handed down to him by his father, once a famous cocker, but now long dead.

Alva went through the gate into the wire-enclosed yard which held about a dozen glossy-feathered young game cocks—"stags" in the parlance of fighting-chicken men. Latching the gate after him, he began to talk to the birds, as was his habit.

"Ah there, Jack," he crooned in an almost tender voice, "it's too bad I've got to hurt you tomorrow. I can't help it though. It's the dubbin' season. All of you boys lose your combs and wattles tomorrow. I've got my dubbin' shears ready. A gamecock has got to get his comb and his lobes and his wattles cut off when he's about five months old, or he can't go into the pit. He'd get all hacked up with them things left on, and the cock that was fightin' him would have an advantage. No sir, it wouldn't do. Every stag has got to have a clean head when he goes into the pit. You'll bleed some, boys, but it won't hurt much. Tomorrow it's got to be done. It's the dubbin' season."

The young stags, strutting about in the August sun, made a wild, strangely colorful picture. As they took to the shade of the clump of elderberry bushes in one corner of the pen, they seemed like a covey of jungle fowls, strangely alien to their middle western environment. The glossy coverts of their wings, their henna hackles, the metallic black of their breasts and the willow green of their legs blended in a lovely, not too bright color scheme. Alva looked on with the eye of a fond admirer. He began to talk to the birds again.

"A prettier bunch I never owned. Pure old Norwood stock, line bred for four years. No man ever had better. Not even the straight John Stone Irish, direct from the originator, was better. Lucky day for me I saw the ad in the old *Game Fowl Monthly* where I could get this stock."

One of the stags, a handsome blackbreasted red, flapped his wings and crowed, a raucous, youthful crow.

"Ah, you rascal," said Alva with pride, "achin' for a fight, are you? Tomorrow you'll get some of that took out of you. Tomorrow you'll get dubbed and your pretty head'll be all bloody. But you'll be glad it's done when you get in the pit for your first battle. It'll hurt tomorrow, but when you have your first scrap you'll be glad your head is smooth and clean so the other cock can't get a billhold too easy."

The stag crowed again and, still smiling to himself, Alva locked the gate to the pen and went up the walk again, his pipe between his teeth and little silvery clouds of tobacco smoke floating behind him.

The next morning Alva was up early, and his breakfast dishes were dried and put in the cupboard behind his rusty cookstove before the mists were above the bayou.

He milked his three cows and turned them into the pasture and scattered ears of corn in his feedlot for the half dozen grunting sows, who had been nuzzling at their trough since dawn. After watering his two horses, he went down the clamshell bordered walk to his chicken pen. Over his arm was a burlap bag, and in one hand a curved pair of nickel-plated surgeon's shears and a huge lump of alum.

At the well, near the chicken yard, he pumped himself a drink of water and grunted with satisfaction as he drained the last few drops of the rusty tin cup. Unlocking the padlock on the gate, he entered the pen and went to the coop which he had locked the night before.

In a moment he emerged with a squawking stag held by the legs. Laying the bird on the burlap bag, he rolled the fowl up in the folds, leaving the bird's head projecting. It resembled the mummy of some sacred bird in its grave trappings.

With the bird's head held in his left hand, its struggling stopped by its burlap bandage, Alva sheared the red comb on the stag's head away, cutting close to the skull. Then he pulled out each wattle and sheared it away close to the bird's throat. The earlobes were then cut away and the head was left, naked and snaky, like that of a turkey vulture. Then he dexterously rubbed the stag's wounds over with a lump of alum to staunch the blood, which was already standing out in great red drops and, unrolling the burlap, he let the frightened bird loose.

"It wasn't so bad, was it, little scrapper?" Alva called out with a laugh, as the stag took refuge in the clump of elderberry bushes.

Another stag was caught and the same operation repeated. Then another and still another was sent scurrying to the elder bush refuge, shorn of his scarlet crown.

So intent was Alva on his bloody work that he did not hear an automobile coming near, nor did he hear footsteps on the walk. It was not until the squeaking of his pump attracted his attention that he looked up. A woman, gray-haired, fashionably gowned, and with a distinguished bearing, was drinking from the rusty cup at the well. Alva's eyes met hers as she hung the cup on the wire hook on the pump. He had just sheared away the comb from a stag and his hands were red with blood. The woman came toward him with a smile, but a quizzical look on her face. Alva arose to his feet. The woman greeted him.

"Good morning, sir," she said. "I've motored through the dust all morning, and was so thirsty I couldn't go any farther without a drink. I saw your pump here and stopped. I'm very much obliged to you."

"You're welcome," said Alva in his colorless voice, wiping his bloody hands on his overall legs.

"But may I ask what you're doing there?" said the woman, with a half frightened, half defiant note in her voice.

Alva shifted from one foot to the other awkwardly; the woman's gaze was on him, and it held a challenge.

Slowly Alva bent over the swathed figure of the fowl and released the bird. It ran away and made a grotesque appearance, with its comb gone, but the red wattles still intact. Alva grew pale. Would this woman understand? Who was she? What could he say?

But there seemed to be no way to begin, so at last he started. "These are fightin' chickens, ma'am. They're stags, us chicken men calls them, and when they're about a year old we, put steel spurs on their spur stubs and fight them against other fellows' birds. Their combs and wattles are in the way then. So we cut 'em off now. That's what we call dubbin'. This is the dubbin' season."

"You mean," almost screamed the woman, "that you cut the combs off the poor creatures and then let them fight each other with steel spurs on their legs?"

"Yes, ma'am," responded Alva with surprise and embarrassment.

"Oh, you brute," shrieked the angry woman before him. "What kind of a beast are you anyway?"

Alva looked at her with astonishment, but before he could answer the woman ran toward the end of the pen where the dubbed stags were huddled together.

"Did you do this to all of these poor things?" shouted the excited woman, pointing an accusing forefinger.

All Alva answered was "Yes, ma'am."

With a cry and a gesture of disgust, the woman whirled on her heel and almost ran toward her car. A moment later Alva watched the shining motor disappear in a cloud of dust down the road.

"Damn funny way to act," grunted Alva to himself.

The next day Alva was cleaning a catfish under the great oak tree in his yard when a stranger stopped in front of his house. The man had an air of brusqueness, and as he greeted Alva with a half grunted "good morning." Alva had a sensation of fear sweep over him. The vision of the gray-haired woman, which had crossed his mind often since the day before, came to him again.

The caller was not long in getting to business.

"You Mr. Alva Whitfield?" he asked.

"Yes," answered Alva simply.

"I'm Gordon Crawley, the constable from Gorge Rapids," said the stranger, pulling at his black mustache, "I've got a warrant for you for cruelty to animals. It's been sworn out by Mrs. Allen Goodhue, president of The Gorge Rapids Humane Society. She says she stopped here yesterday and you was cutting the combs and gills off from roosters, so she drove right in to Gorge Rapids and swore out the warrant for your arrest. Here it is," said the man, pulling a long document from his pocket. "Will you have me read it, or will you waive the readin'?"

"I'll take your word for it," responded Alva. A sickening sensation took possession of him. He reeled and then sat down on a stump.

"Now listen, my friend," said the stranger, with an air of great solicitation, "I'll tell you what you'd better do. This hearin' of yours is to be held in Judge Turner's justice court tomorrow mornin' at ten o'clock. If I was you, I'd plead guilty and pay your fine. There's no use fightin' it. They've got the goods on you. I'll have to take all your chickens along as evidence in court tomorrow, but if you'll promise to appear I'll let it go at that. If you don't appear, of course I'll have to come after you. But I'll trust you. The neighbors around here say you're not a bad fellow. But listen, don't try to fight this. They'll just beat you. Plead guilty and pay your fine and then quit this game chicken business. You can't get by with that stuff any more. I know. I've been in this game too long. I've had too much dealin' with these Prevention of Cruelty cases. It's no use. Plead guilty, pay your fine and then quit. See?"

"Yes," murmured Alva feebly.

"Get your chickens caught. I'll have to take them," said the officer gruffly.

Alva caught the stags and put them in a box and nailed laths across it. Two of the birds stuck their naked and blood-crusted heads out between the pine strips, as Alva carried them down the walk and tied the box on the rear of the Constable's car with a bit of clothesline.

"Now don't forget," said the officer with an attempt at severity. "Be at Judge Turner's court at ten tomorrow morning. So long."

The constable's car went noisily down the road. Alva sank on a stump by the gate. Over the river he could see the heat dancing on the hills, and here and there a green juniper clung to a ledge to break the monotony of the brown slopes.

"Pa said the time would come some day when they'd arrest a man for even keepin' game chickens," muttered Alva to himself. "I didn't believe it."

For a long time he sat on the stump by the roadside. At last he arose and walked slowly to the house. Opening the door, he went through the front room into his tiny bedroom.

From the dark closet he took down the black suit of clothes which he had not worn since Decoration Day. He spread them out on the bed. Then he opened the top drawer of his walnut dresser. Taking out a huge leather pocket wallet, he counted the paper bills he had received for his last year's sale of cordwood.

Slowly he counted:

"Twenty, thirty, forty, fifty. I don't reckon the fine will be more'n that," he muttered with a long sigh.

He replaced the money in the drawer and draped the black suit of clothes over one arm. Walking out of the house, he hung the clothes over the clothesline. Then he walked slowly down the path towards the chicken pen.

At the gate of the pen he stopped. A bloody burlap bag lay on the ground. Feathers scattered here and there and no fowls in sight gave the yard a strange air of loneliness. Alva stood for a long time before the gate, and then turned away and went back toward his white cottage with a slow step. As he plodded along, he dabbed at one eye with a grimy forefinger to remove an imaginary particle of dust.

The Way Out

The last words which William Madsen uttered to his son, Joe, as the death rattle was creeping into this throat were "Work hard, Joe. Study and get registered so you can take care of Ma."

And Joe Madsen had worked hard. Each day the customers in Ordwain's drug store would see the thin, freckled youth as he crushed ice for the soda fountain or waited on customers in the wallpaper section. But three times he had taken the state examination of the Board of Pharmacy, and three times had he failed to get a passing grade.

Then he had made plans for his fourth trip to the State Capitol and the examinations were over again, and once again he was watching the mail.

But one night the fateful letter had come again, informing him of his fourth fruitless attempt.

As he plodded back to the dingy drugstore, it seemed that the end of things had come. He seemed to hear his father's last words ringing in his ears and they sounded like mockery: "Work hard, Joe. Study and get registered so you can take care of Ma."

His face revealed his sorrow, and it was not hidden from the sharp eyes of Mart Ordwain, his employer, who soon asked, as Joe crushed ice at the fountain, "Bad news from the Board, Joe?"

Damn Ordwain! He always seemed to take delight in the troubles of others. But what could you expect from a man who would sell people bad whiskey and then rail at the same people who came into the store later, drunk and empty of pocket.

After the fountain was iced, Joe began mopping up the prescription room of the store. With a heavy heart he dragged the great mop over the splintery floor.

Outside he heard Ordwain talking to the doctor.

"Joe's got bumped again on the state pharmacy examination," Ordwain was saying.

"Well," drawled the doctor, after a long pause, "what else can you expect from a Madsen?"

What else can you expect from a Madsen? The words burned Joe's ear and a great blow seemed to strike him. The mop fell from his hands. He had to lean against the showcase for support. For a long time he stood there with queer sensations tingling up and down his spine.

So this was what was the trouble? He was a Madsen! Never had the idea that his failure might be due to some inherent trait entered his head. He remembered his plodding father only too well and his crippled, old grandfather, who used to live with them and sit day after day in front of house in his faded G.A.R. clothes, but that they might have anything to do with his failures and discouragements had never occurred to him.

He heard his employer leave by the front door. It was the busy season for farmers in the corn country and trade was very light in the drugstore evenings. Each night Ordwain had been going home early and leaving his clerk to close the store by eight o'clock.

For a long time Joe stood by the prescription case, and a tumult of conflicting emotions swept over him. Never had he been so depressed. Despair was in his soul. Why should he suffer so? What was in store for him?

The past came trooping before him. He even remembered such unpleasant things as a beating he once received at the hands of a schoolmate who was two years younger than he. At the time, he had wanted badly to whip his opponent, but his knees had shaken and he had gone down to defeat, though he tried impotently to fight. Now he knew the reason he lost. He was a Madsen!

He felt great drops of sweat breaking out over his forehead. A feeling of nausea came over him. A terrible sinister fear took possession of his being. Why go on with life if one is to be baffled at every turn? He asked himself this question, as he had done often of late.

Two years before, he had taken some insurance in favor of his mother. He thought now what a good thing it might be if he should take ill and die so she could draw the money.

The shelf before him was lined with bottles. One of them was a huge bottle filled with a liquid the color of which could not be seen because of a large label which bore the word *laudanum*.

A convulsive shiver ran over the troubled youth. Laudanum meant sleep, deep sleep, forgetfulness and absolute oblivion, surcease from all trouble and suffering. Again Joe shivered as though from the ague of a swamp dweller.

Swiftly there surged through Joe's brain the events of his life. He seemed to see his father again and his tired mother as she plodded her dull household rounds. Then there coursed through his mind in rapid succession the happenings, one after another, following his father's death. The boy who had administered the thrashing to him in school—he could see him as he stood over him with clenched fists, and he seemed to feel the sting of his blows on his hot cheeks.

His eyes went back again to the bottle. He had heard how old man Carroll, who once practiced law in the town, had been found dead in his room after a protracted debauch, with a bottle of laudanum near his body and a smile on his face.

The thought of his fourth failure in passing the examination for the State Board of Pharmacy rushed back again and smote him with a powerful impact. Again he looked at the bottle. The skull seemed to leer at him from the label, mocking his impotency yet fascinating him with the secret which it guarded. He reached out his hand and touched the stopper and then with a stifled cry, drew his hand back again.

Then another flood of surging, conflicting emotions, and the label on the bottle danced before him. Then again the thought *Here is release!*

Again he was seized with a fit of trembling. Twice again he reached out his hands toward the bottle, but they shook so violently that he let them fall to his side.

At last the thing within him which urged him to grasp the sleep and peace which was within the glass vessel came up again, and this time it did not bring with it the tremor. Groaning and muttering under his breath, Joe seized the stopper of the bottle and wrenching it from the glass neck, he threw it across the room, where it crashed into a row of small vials. With a quick gesture, the large bottle came to his lips, and for a moment he seemed to be locked in a great, black dungeon while he gulped swallow after swallow from the neck of the receptacle which held its gift of death.

It was not until he became aware of a terrible burning within his throat that he stopped his frenzied swallowing. The liquid which he had expected to be bitter yet bland was hot and stung his mouth and throat like fire!

He stopped short and held the bottle before him. The skull on the label leered at him again. He turned the bottle around in his numb, trembling fingers. A smaller label caught his eye. On this smaller label in typed letters were the words *spirits frumenti*. It was Ordwain's private whiskey bottle camouflaged as poison to protect it from loafers who sometimes came behind the prescription case!

Somehow the discovery was a great relief to Joe. He felt no disappointment that his attempt to gain release from his troubles had failed. For some reason which he could not fathom his troubles seemed to have partly vanished! A great joy that he was still living took possession of him!

This was the first time that Joe had ever tasted liquor. Though the fiery stuff had nearly strangled him, he had swallowed quite a quantity of it, and it now sent a delightful sensation through his body. The ecstatic feeling danced down to his very finger tips and coursed down his thighs to his toes. Strange music threaded its lilting way through his brain and he felt like bursting into song. An old tune which his father once played on the violin kept coming to him. He felt a strange strength in his arms, and he seized the mop and began to wield it vigorously.

Up and down the prescription room he went, the water splashing as he kept thrusting the mop into his bucket, and soon the sloshing of the water took a sort of rhythmic measure. He accompanied it with the words of the song which danced in his brain, and his voice rang strange and booming in his own ears.

At last the tune within his head began to drag its course more slowly, and he stopped beside the bottle with its ghostly label. Dropping his mop, he picked up the liquor and drank long and deeply from it again. Then he grabbed up his mop and began to wield it to the lilting cadences of the song which again burst from his lips.

It took Joe longer to mop up the store that night than it ever had taken before. He worked much faster, but he mopped certain places in the floor over and over again to make the task last longer. By the time he had finished, he had gone twice more and tilted the great glass bottle to his lips.

Some twenty minutes later Joe fumbled with the key and at last turned it in the lock of the front door. Turning his face toward home, he lurched back and forth as he went down the sidewalk, and he sang a queer off-key song as he went.

Just before he came to Mart Ordwain's house he spied a shattered watermelon lying in the street where it had fallen from some farmer's wagon. A yell went echoing through the night as Joe reeled to the curb and unsteadily bent over to pick the melon up.

A few minutes later Mart Ordwain was awakened by a loud bump on the side of his house. This noise was followed by a series of wild war whoops which seemed to be coming from someone who passed his house with lurching, unsteady steps.

"Some drunk, I guess," he muttered and turned over and fell asleep again.

Puddles

Morning came to the little Wapsipinicon town of Ontarns in much the same way as age crept on its inhabitants—slowly, with a strange grayness, yet with a sure-footedness that impressed one of a practical thoroughness.

Delbert Montcarn, the storekeeper, for all of the romantic sound of his name, was almost the same color as Ontarns. Clay Street and he matched their environment—even to the morning which was gray with river mists—as a grub fits into the protective color scheme of the old post which houses it in its center.

Delbert Montcarn could not remember that he had ever had a feeling of nostalgia before; in fact, there has never been reason for any periods of homesickness, for he had seldom, in the sixty-eight years of his uneventful life, been away from his natal town except on an occasional visit or a buying trip to Chicago. But today, suddenly and ruthlessly, there was to come to him the first radical change in his life. Today he was leaving Ontarns. The store had been sold, the new proprietor was already in town, and they were moving, he and Ma and Luella, to Gorge Rapids, the county seat and a city of sixty thousand people.

The door of the store opened and broke the reverie into which Delbert had allowed himself to drift, as he sat by the sheet-iron heater near the "candy case" of his general store.

His visitor greeted him with a grunted "Good morning." It was Horace Diltz, postmaster of Ontarns and likewise mayor. Horace and Delbert had pulled in double harness for the good of their native town for many years, and if the town bore scant evidence of their efforts to improve its streets, its buildings and its riverfront, it did not mean that these two somber men and their loyal co-workers had been lacking in enthusiasm.

Horace slumped into a burlap-covered chair opposite Delbert. His face, which was thin and expressionless, was covered with a week's growth of bristles, and except for brownish tobacco stains that reached out from the corners of his sagging mouth, there was little variation in the monotonous grayness of his whole person from the scanty mop of hair protruding from under his ancient felt hat to the frayed laces of his shoes.

"Is this the day you're goin'?" asked Horace. His voice was throaty and the question carried nothing to indicate that there was enough interest back of it to justify its asking.

"Yes," replied Delbert, turning the cigar stub which protruded from his mouth with a deft movement of the tongue, "this is the day. I'm just watchin' the store here for Meigs until he goes to breakfast. He's got possession now. The truck will be here in an hour from Gorge Rapids for our household goods, and Ma and I and Luella will drive in ahead of them and be there in the house to straighten things around. We're comin' back here tomorrow to clean up the house. Meigs is movin' in there, you know, and Ma says she don't want them to move into a dirty place."

"You'll be back here now and then, though?" queried Horace. There was almost a note of plaintiveness in his voice.

"Oh, it may be we'll get out once in a while, but I'm afraid not very often," Delbert answered with a readiness that covered up a strange note in his words. "You see, we'll be pretty busy for a spell. Luella will go right to work and she's goin' to board at home, so Ma will be kind of tied down. Then there'll be a lot for me to look after. I've got some business that I've been puttin' off in Gorge Rapids, and the place we've bought, while it's a good house and all that, needs some fixin' up. The back yard is all sodded, and I want to get that plowed and ready for a garden next spring. Ma wants a trellis put up beside the porch, and if I get time this fall, I want to paint the house. There'll be plenty to keep a fellow busy."

"You know, Delbert," Horace spoke in a low tone and leaned over in his chair toward his friend, "I can't help but think you're makin' a mistake in leavin' Ontarns."

"Why?" Delbert started as though some secret which he had hugged to himself had suddenly been discovered by another.

"Well," drawled Horace, "here you are somebody. This may be a little puddle, but in it you're quite a good-sized toad. Gorge Rapids is a good-size puddle. There a fellow can croak hard and not be heard much."

"Well, but Horace," answered Delbert in a tone that seemed anxious, "I've got something to think of besides myself. I've done good here, I know, and I'm kind of sorry to leave, but what good does it do to educate a girl and then keep her in a place like this? We've worked hard and saved and sent Luella through college and then sent her to business college. She wants to get into the business world, and so I got her this secretary's job in the wholesale house. Ma would never be satisfied to see her go to the city alone, and neither would I. I'll tell you, Horace, it's pretty dull in a place like this for young folks. I can't blame 'em for wantin' to get away. Of course you've managed to keep Alice with you. She took to teachin' and she was lucky and got the home school, but Luella wanted to get into business, and the store here didn't suit her. I don't see no other way out of it but to get her where she's got a chance, and, then, I'm gettin' on in years too. And besides, I've got enough to keep me without workin' any more." This last remark was made in a tone of pride, well suppressed.

"Oh, I know," Horace answered hastily, "you're fixed so you can do it. It wasn't *that* I was thinkin' of. You've always done better than me. I couldn't go to Gorge Rapids and live if I wanted to. I ain't fixed well enough, but I was just thinkin' of all you meant to this community, and what you'd leave, and how you'd miss it, maybe. You've got a good business here. You've been a church leader. You've been mayor of the town. You've been president of the school board. You've been Republican delegate. You've been county supervisor, and I don't know what else. Everybody knows you for miles around. You stand ace-high with everyone. It takes years to build up a reputation like you've got, and when a man's your age he don't make acquaintances as fast as a younger man.

That's what I was thinkin' of."

The two men remained silent for a few moments, but the swinging of the door interrupted their thoughts and a girl of perhaps twenty years entered the store. She was dressed in a fashionable though rather shoddy frock, and her closely-cropped blond hair was waved in the latest mode. Laughter was in the blue eyes, and though her cheeks were over-rouged and her lips too scarlet for real freshness, there was a certain prettiness of feature that seemed strangely out of place against the somber background of the cluttered old store.

"Pa, why aren't you coming to breakfast?" said the girl in her high-pitched voice.

"I'm waitin' for Meigs to come back," answered her father in the tone men use when they are in the presence of domineering members of their household.

"Oh, hang Meigs," said the girl impatiently. Lock the dump up. I'd think you'd had enough of this. Do you know," this to Horace, "Pa has been mooning around like he was homesick. I almost believe he hates to leave this burg!"

"How about *you*, Luella?" asked Horace in his colorless tone.

"*Me?*" The girl broke into laughter. "Why I'm floating in air, I'm that tickled. Say, Mr. Diltz," said the girl in her nervous accents, "do you know the last week has seemed like an age to me. I simply can't stand it here any longer. I'm sick of the town, sick of the faces, sick of the very songs they sing in the church. The sight of that river on a morning like this makes me shudder. I guess I never was cut out to live in a small town. I told my girlfriend in Gorge Rapids a few days ago that it was funny how I never took to this place. It's mighty strange, my being born and raised here, too. But from the time I was old enough to realize anything, I've always wanted to get out of here and go to the city. Of course I stood it until now, but Pa is getting old and Ma ought to have a better house, and after I came home from Gorge Rapids, I just put my foot down and insisted that the folks had to get out of here. Lord, I'd die if I couldn't get away."

"Alice is quite contented here," said Horace feebly. It seemed he could offer no other defense to the girl's indictment of the town.

"Oh, I know," answered Luella. "Alice is very happy here, and I'm so glad, but," she patted her blond hair at the temples, "Alice is quite a different person. She and I are much different in temperament. Alice is quieter. She is satisfied with the commonplace. As for me, well," the girl broke into laughter again, "I guess there's a sort of romantic streak in me, though for the life of me I don't know where it could come from, but I love cities. I crave something exciting. I simply can't stand the humdrum existence of a place like this. I'm going into business, not because I'm so much in love with business, but because business means the city and the city means people—lots of people, and where there's people, things happen, and, when things happen, life has color—but," looking toward her father, "Pa and Ma find it hard to understand me. It's no wonder. I'm so different from them."

The two old men walked toward the door. The young woman followed them. At the door they met a man who, though he was well past middle age, looked young and his clothes were suggestive of the city. He paused to take the key to the door from Delbert Montcarn. Awkwardly Delbert introduced him to his daughter as Mr. Meigs, the new proprietor of the store.

Meigs acknowledged the introduction with an easy friendliness and took in Luella from head to foot with a swift glance of appraisal.

"Well, Miss Montcarn," he said laughingly, "here you go to Gorge Rapids while I come from Gorge Rapids to take your place in Ontarns. Your father tells me you do not regret leaving here."

"Quite the contrary," laughed Luella. "I'm glad to go, to fill up the place you leave in the great city."

"Well," answered Meigs, "Good luck! I'm glad, for my part, to get away from the city. I come from a long line of farmer folk, and as I grew older I felt an urge to get back to a place like this. I nearly went on a farm, but finally compromised on this store. I'm going to be satisfied here, I'm sure. I hope you will be, with your new life in the city."

The two old men walked on ahead. For a moment they were both silent. At last Horace Diltz spoke.

"There's something I can't understand. There's a man who's always lived in a big city comin' here to this small town, and here you're leavin' here and goin' to the city. I can't make it out. His folks, he says, was country folks. Now he feels like gettin' back to the country again. But your folks was here before you, Delbert, and here's your daughter wantin' to get out of here and get to a bigger place. It's more'n I can understand, unless it's some kind of a throwback. Somewhere there must of been some of your folks that was in big puddles."

The two men parted at Delbert Montcarn's gate.

"I'll be in to see you before I go," said Delbert as they parted.

Mrs. Montcarn met her husband and daughter at the door. Her ample form was clad in a gingham dress and a "dust-cap" was above her perspiring, round face. As they crossed the door sill, she sank into a rocker and addressed her husband:

"Pa, I wish you'd look over everything in the attic before we go. There's loads of trash up there in them old trunks your mother left, and I don't believe we want to take any of it with us. But you look it all over. The trunks ain't been touched since your mother died."

Slowly Delbert Montcarn climbed the stairs which led up to the dusty attic. It had been a number of years since he had visited the musty old room above the rooms where he had lived so many years. He was the youngest of five children and the only one of the family surviving. His mother had died under his roof at an advanced age, and her few poor effects, including two ancient battered trunks, had been stored at her son's house since her death.

Delbert had never really known his mother. She had seemed, outwardly, much like the other farmers' wives in the neighborhood, but her silence, which was broken only on rare occasions, covered well her real self, and the shy soul of her youngest son had never broken beyond the wall of it.

Delbert stood for a long time over one of the ancient trunks. At last he lifted the lid, showering dust on the pine floor as he did so.

The trunk was full of old dresses, old books, two or three family albums and some newspapers yellowed with age. Delbert rummaged among the musty things. One album was filled with tintypes of people dressed in garments long gone out of fashion, and the styles of beards and hairdress made even the somber storekeeper smile. As he turned the pages, he came upon a yellowed envelope. The address was so faded as to be almost illegible, and even the postmark was blurred from age.

Delbert inserted a soiled forefinger into the envelope and drew out the letter. It was yellowed and faded too, but not so much but it could be easily made out. The writing was a woman's, and Delbert saw that it was a message written to his mother by his grandmother. The letter said:

> Dear Daughter:
>
> I received your note, and I make haste to answer. Do not, I beg of you, do as you say you feel like doing. Your husband is a splendid man and though he is only a farmer, as your own father was, he is a man who is worthy of you, a man of principle, and thrifty. I know how you dislike the life of a farmer's wife, and how you long for the city, as I once did. But this, my daughter, you will get over, and in time you will learn to make the most of your lot, as I have done. Remember your child. Be silent and remember that as the wife of your husband, you are a person of some note among your neighbors. I find that discontent is in the hearts of many people. It is not alone the farm folk who feel it. How do you know that you would lose it in the city? To leave your husband will only bring unhappiness to him and disgrace to you.
>
> Your Mother

For a long time Delbert Montcarn sat and held the yellowed sheets in his hand. In his eyes was a look which comes to the eyes of one who only half understands a newfound truth, but who accepts and gropes no farther.

"Horace was right," he muttered. "It's a throwback. That's what makes 'em want to get into big puddles, and sometimes when they're there, makes 'em want to get out."

Up the stairway came Luella's high-pitched voice.

"Hurry up, Pa, the truck's here!"

The Runaway

Hinton Fenmore surveyed the empty fruit jars that stood on the oilcloth-covered kitchen table. After standing over the remains of what had been an enthusiastic beginning of a peach-canning campaign, Hinton walked across the kitchen where two unopened baskets of great yellow "lemon cling" peaches stood by the wall. Another basket, nearly empty, stood near, and above him on the pantry shelves were arranged six newly filled jars. The golden slices lay with a studied evenness inside the glass. Lavina did all her canning so. She had something of the artist about her which showed even in the way she hung a washing on her line each Monday. The contrast between Lavina and her uncouth husband was something which the neighbors had long commented upon.

Two days before Hinton had driven to Gorge Rapids for three bushels of peaches. Lavina had insisted that he do so, for never in the twenty years which she had lived with Hinton on the little sterile farm by the Wapsipinicon had winter found their cellar barren of an abundance of canned fruit.

But this year had, for a time, threatened to be an exception. Always pressed hard to pay the interest on his mortgage and the taxes on the farm, this year, with its scourges and corn crop failure, had made the farmers along the ridge road poorer than ever, and Hinton had been forced to curtail expenses in every possible way, and his continued admonitions to Lavina had caused even more bickerings than usual. Lavina had at last been able to show Hinton that to put up the usual amount of fruit was a form of economy, rather than an expenditure for luxuries. It had not been easy to convince him, but, without a verbal surrender, he had suddenly made it plain that he was going, on a certain day, to Gorge Rapids, and on the morning he started, Lavina had, by subtle suggestion, given him instructions about the peaches.

She had learned to know Hinton Fenmore well. To come out bluntly and give him orders was usually to court failure. To coax too much would have been revealing a certain weakness, but to clip an advertisement from the Gorge Rapids *Times*, which announced that the Gorge Fruit Company had three carloads of peaches on track, and then to hand him the clipping just before he left, without comment, was a bit of finesse which could only be known to one who has lived two decades with a man used to fighting stubborn river silt long and unsuccessfully.

But the night Hinton had returned from Gorge Rapids he had come with something besides the peaches. Years ago when every town along the Wapsipinicon harbored a saloon, Hinton and Lavina had often been near to parting. She had come from over the "Arp's Ridge" way, where the church was the main social institution of the neighborhood. Hinton was a Fenmore and a Fenmore either drank or had "quit." Hinton had never formally announced his intention to quit until one day Lavina had packed her few clothes in a shabby valise and gone back to her father's home on Arp's Ridge. Everyone remembered that since she had returned to Hinton, he had seldom been seen in a saloon and had even moved out of his old neighborhood to get away from his old drinking cronies.

But the night he returned from Gorge Rapids, Lavina had noticed him lurch slightly as he unhitched his team, and as she peered out of the window, she saw him slyly secrete a brown jug in the oat bin. He lingered longer than usual at his chores that night, and when he had come in with the first basket of peaches, after his milking was done, it was to face a broadside of denunciations from the angry Lavina.

Made brave by the liquor, Hinton retaliated. Then there had been a period of sulking on the part of Lavina followed with a further quarrel the next morning, and when, on that day, Hinton had returned from the field at noon, he found the house deserted and though he called again and again there was no response from his wife.

Hinton walked about the room several times and then stepped out the door. The day was almost perfect with the first touch of that haze that announces fall. The ragweeds along the road were grey with dust, and the hills across the Wapsipinicon were brown but for an occasional touch of dark green where a juniper clung to a limestone ledge.

"Lavina!"

Hinton's voice echoed through the maple grove, and two hens, dusting themselves at the base of the giant cottonwood, ran away in wild confusion. "Lavina!" again he called and his voice quavered. The only answer was the crowing of the barred cock near the barn.

There was the sound of wheels down the lane and a decrepit top buggy appeared. Seated in it were two men, one a stocky middle-aged fellow in overalls, the other an older man with a scraggly grey beard.

"Find her yet? called out the stocky man by way of salutation.

"No," whimpered Hinton, "ain't this tough, boys? I guess she's gone for good and it's usin' me just right. She's too good for me anyway."

Hinton wiped his eyes on the back of his grimy hand.

"Art and Hosey'll be over in a few minutes," said the stocky man. "We let them know just as soon as you telephoned, and they'll be right over. We'll have to drag the river, I guess. You can't tell what a woman her age might do. She was about forty-five, wasn't she?"

"Yes, but boys, I can't think she's jumped in the river," said Hinton, quaveringly.

"You can't tell," said the older man, "look at what Jim Catless's woman done. She got on a tantrum and cut her throat with a butcher knife. She was just Lavina's age."

The hoofbeats of another team were heard. Another top buggy came up the lane through the maples. Two men, one a thin, bony farmer with a walrus mustache and fast working jaws, the other a somber individual of about thirty, called out "hellos" as the team reined in.

"Hosey, I was just tellin' Hinton, we'd probably have to drag the river," said the stocky man. "I hate to make old 'Hint' feel bad but I'm afraid there's where we'll find her."

He looked toward Hinton, who was wiping his eyes again.

"It's hell, boys," said Hinton as he wept great tears. "It seems I've had about all the tough luck a man can stand. I'm way behind, and I got two notes due at the bank. My taxes and interest ain't paid. Now to have this happen is about too much." Hinton's voice trailed off into a near wail.

"Oh, buck up, 'Hint'," said the stocky man with an attempt at light-heartedness, "it maybe won't be so bad. I ain't saying she's jumped in the river but she might. Let's get to lookin'. The thing is to get her located."

"It's all my fault," went on Hinton, not to be turned away from his grief. "What business did I have to go to drinkin' again? After layin' off for years, then why did I have to buy that jug of ripsaw? Of course I had been blue and worried, but I knowed how against it she was and why did I have to stir her up? She was a damn good woman," he finished chokingly.

"Well, let's get goin'," said the stocky man. "Let's hitch our teams and go down the river and look for tracks."

As the men tied their teams to nearby maples, Hinton drew a great red bandana from his overall pocket and mopped his face. Replacing the bandana, he tugged at his mustache and looked across the river to the brown hills beyond.

The four men came toward him and the stocky man was in the lead.

"Have you got a trotline and some big catfish hooks?" he asked the somber visaged Hinton.

"Yes, what do you want them for? asked Hinton, his bewildered expression giving his wrinkled face a grotesque appearance that was almost comical.

"To make a drag with. We'll take your boat and drag up and down the river, and if she's there the hooks'll ketch in her dress."

Hinton gasped.

"God, don't say that," he said in a shaking voice.

"The men walked slowly toward the barn, Hinton leading. Suddenly he stopped.

"Boys, I'm pretty shaky," he said in a low voice. "Don't you think it might nerve us up to take a little drink all around?" There was a note of something between eagerness and terror in his voice.

The stocky man slowed his gait. "It's kind of a spooky business, draggin' a river," he said in a low tone.

Hinton turned his course toward the granary. Outside the door he stopped suddenly. Then he turned and, looking at his companions, he pointed silently to the ground where lay the fragments of a shattered jug. The men stared at the wreckage.

"She's found my jug," said Hinton, "she's found it and smashed it!"

At that moment he chanced to look toward the house and he saw a woman's face peering out between the parted curtains of an upstairs window.

Before the face could be withdrawn, Hinton grasped the sleeve of the stocky man and pointed toward the house.

"Look!" he shouted, "a fine trick to play on a feller!"

A grin spread over the stocky man's face. He turned to his three companions.

"Let's just ease away, boys, and never let on," he told the others. Then turning to Hinton, "Just go along as if nothin' ever happened to your jug. She'll be all right now. You can't tell nothin' about 'em at that age. They're liable to do most anything, but just go on out to the field. She'll likely have supper ready when you come in tonight. She'll be satisfied just bustin' your jug. Don't tell me—I know 'em."

Bitter Herbs

Grandma Giltner came out of the thicket along the railroad track and struck her rusty spade against a fence post to dislodge the yellow clay that clung to its flanks. Streams of perspiration trickled down her wrinkled old cheeks, and here and there across the back of her faded blue calico dress was a damp spot where the moisture of her shriveled old body had soaked through. Her breath came in gasps and the words that flowed in a low mumbling were lost.

Following at her heels came Ottie Holt, a neighbor's son, and he carried a great hickory-splint basket on his arm filled to the top with roots and black cherry bark.

"Let's sit down and rest, Granny," said the boy, but the old woman had already dropped down on the grass under a linden tree.

"Give me the basket," said Grandma Giltner between gasps.

The boy sat down beside the old woman and rubbed his bare legs with a grimy hand to relieve the nettle stings.

Grandma Giltner emptied part of the contents of the basket on the ground and began to sort them, muttering to herself as she did so.

"Here's mandrake; good for gall trouble. Here's bloodroot for my tonic. Here's golden seal; good for canker sores. Here's wild anise; good for flavorin' my cough medicine. Here's wild onion; that goes in my cough medicine, too. Here's wild cherry bark; good for consumption."

The boy gazed at the old woman in open-eyed wonder. Ever since he could remember anything, old Grandma Giltner had lived in the tiny sheet-iron covered shanty in the edge of the little Wapsipinicon village of Ontarns, and the people of the crossroads town and the country, too, for that matter, held her in awe.

Although her reputation had grown as she became more bent and shriveled with the years, she still was as silent and somber as ever, and her little shack was seldom visited by anyone. Even the patients who called the old woman, though they seldom paid her anything, usually telephoned to the grocery store that she was wanted or sent a boy in the family. They seemed to prefer that Granny keep all her secrets to herself and hold an air of mystery about her methods.

Granny and the boy who plodded with her parted at the sagging gate in front of her shanty. For a long time the old woman sat on a great granite boulder that lay in her dooryard. The basket of roots and herbs was beside her. Around the eaves of the little porch, which fringed her tiny dwelling, hung bound festoons of thoroughwort, smartweed, mullein and dried burdock root. It was late summer and Granny was ready for the autumn, for her stock of curative barks, roots, and herbs was complete.

A puff of dust showed around the bend of the road and a shiny Ford car came into sight. It was driven by Doctor Wold, the young physician in Ontarns. Doctor Wold halted his car by Granny's gate and alighted.

"Mrs. Giltner, may I have some water for my radiator?" asked Dr. Wold, raising his hat.

"There's the pump," growled the old woman, hardly glancing up.

"Fine weather we're having," commented Dr. Wold as he walked by her with a dripping bucket.

"Fine for milk-sickness," answered Granny in her same irritable voice.

Dr. Wold smiled a wry smile and made no reply. After filling the radiator of his car he returned the bucket to the well platform and started toward the gate.

"Thank you, Mrs. Giltner," called out Dr. Wold.

The old woman made no answer, but her eyes followed the physician as he strode down the path. Near the gate he paused to admire a clump of hollyhocks that were just reaching the height of their blooming.

"You have some lovely old flowers in your garden." said the doctor.

Granny ignored the remark, and a strange light burned in her sunken old eyes. As Dr. Wold placed his hand on the latch of the gate, she arose and picked up her basket, calling out in a voice that was cracked with a queer suppressed laughter, "Who you goin' to kill today?"

Dr. Wold tried to smile, but the attempt was a poor one. As his car moved away from the gate he muttered, "No use trying to make friends with that old witch."

Dr. Wold had had encounters with Granny before. Once he had gone far back on the ridge road to see a patient and had arrived there to find Granny firmly established with the ailing man, who was well in a few days. Dr. Wold's bill was never paid, and the simple farmer lost no opportunity, when in a crowd, to tell how Granny had thrown the doctor's medicine in the hog pen and given spikenard tea instead. This story enhanced her reputation all the more.

Another time, after a patient far back along the river had passed the crisis in pneumonia, Granny had been called by an ignorant hired girl, and the man was dosed with great drafts of hot cherry bark tea. When the half delirious farmer was himself, he refused to let Dr. Wold see him again.

On the other hand, while Granny was given credit for many marvelous cures by the river valley people, she was never blamed for a death. The wise old woman was usually called after a physician was discharged or had made at least one visit. When she came into the sick room her first question always was "Has he had any medicine?"

If the patient had taken anything in the way of drugs, the old woman would ask to see them. Then she would taste the medicine, smell it, front, and say, "It's a wonder it didn't kill him. Throw it out. I don't know whether I can save him or not. He's too full of poison!"

Or, if no doctor had been present, she would say, "Why didn't you send for me sooner? It's got too much of a start. You haven't given me no chance. I don't know whether I can help him or not."

Granny sat in the yard for a long time. Once she drew her old clay pipe out of her apron pocket, put it in her mouth, but returned it to the apron pocket again without filling it.

Suddenly another cloud of dust appeared down the road. This time it was a man on horseback, and she recognized the rider as Jake Lower, the cattle buyer.

Jake reined his horse at the gate.

"Granny," the red-faced cattle buyer called out, "they want you out to Ed Sickle's place."

"What's up?" asked Granny calmly.

"His girl's awful sick, and Ed's in bed with a broken leg," replied Jake.

Granny sighed. Jake did not wait for an answer. He knew that Ed Sickle was in the habit of calling Granny, and he knew, too, that Granny never failed to respond when word was sent to her.

It was three miles back in the hills on Big Creek to Ed Sickle's home. Granny had often been here. She remembered well when Ed's little girl had been born. Ed's wife had died, but the child lived, and the lonely, improvident Ed Sickle seem to exist only for the shy, frail girl who was now twelve years old.

Granny hobbled into her house and changed her faded dress to another, clean but equally faded. Before the little cracked mirror which hung beneath her clock shelf, she brushed back the sparse yellowish-white hair and adjusted her old black bonnet. Her cat mewed and rubbed his black sides against her leg, but she paid no attention. In a few minutes she was plodding down the dusty road toward Big Creek, her old leather valise of herbs dangling from a strap which crossed her bent shoulders.

Ed Sickle shouted "come in" when Granny knocked on the door of his house. Inside she found the tall, blond, farmer stretched out in one of the two ill-furnished bedrooms, and his twelve-year-old daughter talking in a delirium from the other room.

The littered kitchen, its table loaded with dirty dishes, egg shells, and bread crusts, told how the girl had struggled against her sickness, playing the dual role of nurse and houeskeeper while her strength waned.

The farmer tried to smile when he saw Granny enter.

"I'm up against it, Granny," he called out. "This here broken leg has got me nailed down. Gracie done the best she could, and she'd made it all right, but she took down yesterday. I couldn't get out to send no word until a neighbor dropped in this mornin'. I'm 'fraid the kid's bad off."

"I'll see," responded Granny as she removed her bonnet.

"Don't pay no attention to me. Give it all to Gracie," said Sickle in a choking voice.

The old woman cleared off the top of the rusty stove and filled an iron kettle with water from a tin pan in the sink. Then with corncobs and dry wood she started a fire.

Not until the kettle was set on the stove did she go into the bedroom.

"Can you let me see your tongue, Gracie?" she said to the girl in a gentle tone.

The girl's eyes stared glassily, and she clutched at the folds of her torn and soiled nightgown.

The old woman stood by the bed for a long time. Then she took her old leather satchel from a chair and dropped several handfuls of dried herbs into the kettle of water.

The house was oppressively hot. Outside the sun beat down, but was suddenly blotted out by a great inky cloud. Far away a long trembling peal of thunder sounded. The maples in the dooryard showed the silver lining of their leaves.

Granny went again to the bedroom. The girl was sitting up and staring before her and motioning with one hand, as though counting objects on the wall.

The old woman tried to get the child to lie down. She paid no heed when Granny tried to force her back on the pillow, but struggled when the old woman used more strength in an attempt to force her back.

In the other room, Ed Sickle groaned from weariness and pain. Once he called Granny.

"How is she, Granny?" he asked anxiously.

"Bad, Ed," was all the old woman said.

The kettle on the stove was boiling. Granny poured some of the greenish fluid into a bowl and set it by the window to cool. Outside the sky grew blacker. The peals of thunder came nearer and the approach of night saw the storm gathering rapidly.

Granny went again to the bedroom.

The girl was sitting on the edge of the bed talking incoherently. Again Granny tried to force her to lie down. The child struggled and sobbed and finally lay back on the pillow exhausted.

The old woman retraced her steps and stirred the contents of the kettle. Then she tasted the greenish liquid from the bowl beside the window. She could hear Ed Sickle groaning again in his room.

Going into the bedroom, Granny found Gracie on the floor, mumbling and picking at a knot in the pine boards. The old woman pleaded with her.

"Gracie, get back in bed. Here, Gracie, I've brought you some medicine. Here, girl, take it. "

At last she got the child on the bed. Touching her temple she found the fever raging, and she could feel the girl's heart pounding as though driven by some devilish force.

Gracie now lay still, but the old woman's attempts to make her swallow the medicine were futile.

Granny went to the door. Rain was falling in torrents and a stiff wind bent the dooryard trees. It was nearly dark.

The old woman went into the farmer's room.

"How's she?" he asked anxiously.

Granny only shook her head and went again into the kitchen. Taking up the bowl of medicine, she entered the girl's room again. This time she struggled fiercely in a vain attempt to force some of the bitter potion between the girl's hot, dry lips.

Outside, the storm gave no promise of abating. Lightning flashed in one yellow, jagged gash after another and the darkness had grown inky. The thunder roared continuously.

The old woman seated herself near the door and rested her head in her hands. For a long time she sat silently. Between the peals of thunder she could hear Gracie's delirious babbling.

At last Granny arose and lit a kerosene lamp. The girl was quiet for a moment. The old woman tiptoed into her room and saw the child's eyes were closed and her mouth was gaping open. Her chest was rising and falling with labored breathing. Silently, Granny stole into the room with the bowl of medicine in her hand. Stealthily, she moved to the bedside and dropped a little of the medicine between the girl's open jaws.

Grace choked and spluttered and turned on her side. The few drops of greenish liquid spilled over the pillow. A peal of thunder drowned the child's screams.

Granny hurried from the room and seized her old bonnet from a nail by the door. Hurrying to the door of Sickle's room, she called out:

"Ed, I'm goin' to town. There's somethin' I've got to get. I'll be back as soon as I kin!"

She heard Sickle call to her, but a peal of thunder drowned his words.

Out into the blinding storm the frail old woman beat her way. The wind had subsided somewhat, but the rain was falling in great sheets. Down the road she forced her path, her feet slipping in the hill clay, her old calico dress clinging to her bony frame.

It was more than three miles to Ontarns and most of the way the storm beat on the old woman with all its late summer fury. Many times Granny was hurled to the ground, and once in sheer exhaustion she lay by the roadside for what seemed hours, but the muscles in her toothless old jaws never relaxed until she dragged her drenched form up to the gate above which hung an illuminated sign: DR. WOLD, PHYSICIAN AND SURGEON.

Sleepily, Dr. Wold answered the furious rappings on his front door, and he gasped with amazement when he beheld the bedraggled Grandma Giltner at his threshold. Before he could speak, Granny said breathlessly, "Can your new car make mud like this?"

"Of course, but come in. You're drenched. Let me get you a change of clothes. Mrs. Wold is your size. Here, sit down. You're almost exhausted.

The old woman's eyes shot out strange glints.

"There's someone three miles up on Big Creek that's lots worse off than me, and if you don't want to come, and come quick, I'm off to Ludeville for another doctor," cried Granny in her shrill voice.

Dr. Wold hurried into his clothes as the old woman filled her pipe from the tobacco jar on his table. When he returned fully dressed, he brought a coat for her, which she allowed him to wrap about her after many protests.

On the way to the Big Creek neighborhood the doctor tried, as he fought his way from side to side of the slippery road, to learn all he could of the case upon which he had been so unceremoniously summoned, but Granny was noncommittal. All she would say was "I don't know. I thought it was her liver. It acts queer. Maybe you'll know, and then maybe you won't!"

When the doctor stopped at the door of Ed Sickle's farmhouse, the old woman paid no heed to his attempts to help her alight from the car, but crawled out and led the way into the bedroom where Gracie Sickle lay. The girl was quieter now. The doctor made a hasty examination and muttered, apparently to himself as he turned away:

"Scarlet fever. A bad case aggravated by lack of care."

Skillfully he ministered to the sick girl. The old woman watched him with her hawklike eyes. Several times the doctor turned and asked Granny to assist him.

She held his fever thermometer; she brought him hot water. She was fascinated by the neat array of bottles in his medicine case.

When the child was attended to, the doctor went into the father's room.

The gaunt farmer was crying softly to himself, spent with anxiety over his daughter.

"Nevermind, Ed," said Dr. Wold, "she's pretty sick, but we'll bring her out, won't we, Mrs. Giltner?"

Granny smiled a toothless smile.

"I've never paid you, Doc, for the time you sewed up my foot when I chopped it," whimpered Sickle.

The doctor gave a reassuring sweep of the hand and silenced the worried farmer.

"Now, Ed," continued Dr. Wold, "Mrs. Giltner will stay here until morning. The girl's pretty sick, but I've fixed her up so she'll be all right that long. In the morning I'll come out and bring help. Mrs. Giltner had better not stay. It will be too stiff for her with you both in bed."

The doctor started for the door after going back into Gracie's room.

At the door he paused to give instructions to Granny. The storm had quieted and the moon was showing through a tattered span of cloud.

Granny followed the doctor outdoors.

"Go back, Mrs. Giltner, and dry your clothes," he coaxed.

"I want to ask you somethin'," said the old woman.

The doctor paused.

Granny hesitated and then said, "When you come out tomorrow, will you take me back with you? And when I pack up some things will you take me over to Knowlport?"

"Of course I will, Mrs. Giltner," answered Dr. Wold good-naturedly, "but why are you going to Knowlport?"

"My son lives there," replied Granny. "He's been wantin' me to come and live with him for a long time. I guess I'll go. He wants me, and I'm gettin' old—too old for doctorin'."

The Old Order Changeth

The stairway leading up to the attic in the old Groves house was spread with a thick coat of dust, for the tenants on the Groves farm had never been sufficiently curious to investigate these haunts of moth and mouse and climb up the steep incline which led to the gloomy, low-ceiling room above the kitchen.

Old Roscoe Groves, the owner of the farm, groaned and clutched his rheumatic hip as he pushed up the trap door and stood at last in the attic. It was twenty years since he had last been up there. He remembered exactly. It was the fall that he moved to California. A long time! Oh, no, not so long when you look back, but a long time when you look ahead. Roscoe had heard his father say this.

He groped for the window shade. It flew up causing him to start violently, and a cloud of grayish dust went across the room in circling wreaths. There was plenty of light now, and Roscoe seated himself in an old splint-bottomed chair near the horsehair trunk. The sweat trickled down his spare, pale cheeks. It was like a furnace in the little attic, for the July sun beat relentlessly on the roof.

Suspended from a rafter was a motley collection of old clothing; an old soldier overcoat with a gray, paper-like wasp's nest attached to the collar, a beaded gown that had been Sarah's. It was the only piece of extravagance she had ever been guilty of. His wife, Sarah, had sold her turkeys on a high market that fall.

Roscoe sighed. Somehow the ordeal of looking over the old familiar things in the attic was a greater one than he had anticipated. Maybe he should have waited longer. Sarah had been dead only two years. But he had felt brave enough and so he had come. Tomorrow he was going back to California. He turned toward a mass of rubbish in the corner. An old harness. A birdcage. An old saddle, and of all things in the world—the old dulcimer he had played on at country dances, along the Wapsipinicon, nearly fifty years ago!

A wry half-smile came to Roscoe's lips. It had been years since he had even thought of a dulcimer. This queer, homemade substitute for a piano had once charmed him, and the flush of pride he once felt when he used to seat himself by the fiddler at a dance came back to him like a subdued, warm glow.

Roscoe heard a step on the stair and looking around he saw a blond curly head appear through the trap door. At once he recognized the six-year-old daughter of Miller, his farm tenant. When he drove into the yard, he had seen her playing with her dolls under the great cottonwood by the gate. She put her foot on the last step and shyly walked toward the old man.

"What are you looking at?" the little girl asked.

What was he looking at? Roscoe did not immediately answer. He scarcely knew himself why he had sought this dusty attic on this hot afternoon. He looked toward the dulcimer.

"I'm looking at the dulcimer," answered Roscoe, hardly knowing what he had said.

"What's a dulcimer?" naively queried the little girl.

Roscoe smiled. Then for a moment he was lost in reverie.

Again: "What's a dulcimer?"

The old man turned on his chair and looked at the child. She expected an answer. There was no question about that.

"Why, didn't anybody ever tell you what a dulcimer was?" asked Roscoe.

"No," answered the child simply.

The old man arose painfully from the chair and hobbled toward the pile of rubbish. Bending over, he picked up the dusty old instrument. A mouse scampered from the opening in front of the dulcimer. Tied to one pair of strings were the tiny wooden mallets with which the musician beat the pairs of strings when he played the chords to a lilting dance tune. Roscoe sat down and blew the dust from the polished black face of the instrument. Then fumblingly he untied the mallets from the strings. The child watched with rapt attention.

"This, I used to play at dances," explained Roscoe. As he said this he strummed on the ancient strings with his fingers. The child laughed as the tinkling sounds escaped them.

Old Roscoe sat silent for a time.

"Play a tune," the child coaxed.

The old man thought for a moment. Then suddenly his gnarly old fingers tightened on the mallets, and he began beating out the notes of an old dance tune. As he played a smile came to his bloodless lips. Suddenly his head went back and the words of an old dance echoed toward the rafters.

"Allemande left!"

The child laughed again and clapped her hands.

"Grand right and left!"

Old Roscoe's hands were swimming over the strings, and the rollicking dance tune came with its tinny cadences like the wind's breath through the ice-covered weeds after a night of sleet.

"Honor your partner!"

The child began to dance, and the dust flew in a cloud toward the ceiling.

Suddenly a mouse darted from a pile of old clothing and ran near the child's feet. She suddenly ceased dancing, and a startled cry escaped her. Old Roscoe stopped his playing, and the child crouched near an old chest until the mouse disappeared under a stack of newspapers.

There was a step on the stair, and the surly face of Miller, the tenant on the farm, appeared. He looked at his little daughter in surprise and then at Roscoe.

"I've been waitin' for a half hour, Mr. Groves. I want you to look over that seedin'. I want you to look over the barn floor, too. It needs fixin'."

"Yes. I'll be right down, Miller," said the old man sheepishly.

"Go on down, Gertie," said Miller to his little daughter.

The child obeyed with a glance at old Roscoe.

"I've been playing a little tune on the dulcimer for your little girl," explained the old man.

"I don't like to have her up here among these dirty things," growled the tenant. "There's danger she might get some disease."

Miller had started down the ladder, and old Roscoe followed him painfully. Once outdoors the tenant led the way and Roscoe trailed after.

"I used to play the dulcimer at dances," explained the older man.

The sullen look on Miller's face melted somewhat.

"That was a good while ago, I guess," he muttered as he opened the gate for Roscoe to enter the stubble field.

"About fifty years," said Roscoe.

"Folks don't care much for them old-time dances," said the tenant. "They dance 'em different now. What did you say that thing you was playin' was called?"

"A dulcimer. You see they played them . . ."

Miller interrupted. "I've seen it up there but didn't know what it was. Nobody uses them any more, I guess. They want orchestra music now."

"It was mighty pretty music, a fiddle and a dulcimer," said old Roscoe as he laboriously hobbled through the stubble.

Miller was examining the ground.

"Now here, Mr. Groves," he was saying, "you see this new seedin' didn't ketch. It's got to be seeded again."

"How much will it cost?" asked old Roscoe with a note of sadness in his voice.

"Oh, about sixty dollars, I guess," said the tenant unfeelingly, "but it's got to be done."

"Couldn't it wait until next year?" feebly asked old Roscoe. "I've got so much expense."

"No, it can't. People don't put things off that way nowadays. It don't pay."

"Well, I suppose then it'll have to be done," old Roscoe sighed.

They closed the gate and went toward the horse barn. Standing in the door, the tenant pointed to the floor.

"It will have to be cemented," he explained.

"How much do you reckon that will cost?" the old man asked querulously.

"About seventy-five dollars," was Miller's quick response.

"I suppose lumber wouldn't be cheaper?" asked old Roscoe in a monotone.

"Not much and it's no good," quickly answered Miller. "They don't do that anymore with horse barns. It don't pay."

The two men went up the walk to the house. Both of them scraped their feet on the iron scraper outside the door. Miller held the door open and motioned for the old man to enter. Inside he pointed to the massive plush-covered rocker.

The tenant's wife came in from the kitchen and wiped her hands on her calico apron.

"Dinner'll be ready in a minute," she said. Her florid face dripped perspiration.

"Hadn't you better ask Mr. Groves about that sink?" asked Miller guardedly.

"Why yes, I nearly forgot. The sink needs re-linin' and needs a new pipe, too. It's caused a lot of trouble."

For a moment old Roscoe did not answer and when he finally did his voice seemed strangely quavering.

"About how much . . ."

"I had Lurton the hardware man out here, and he looked at it and said it would be eleven dollars," replied Mrs. Miller with alacrity.

There was a pause. Old Roscoe pulled his thin, gray mustache. At last he said, "No way you could get along with it the way it is until I get some expense out of the way?"

"It would be dangerous. Folks can't take chances nowadays. It might pollute the well, and I ain't goin' to be runnin' outdoors emptyin' water all winter this year." Mrs. Miller stopped with an air of finality.

Old Roscoe merely nodded.

Miller had gone over and turned on the radio which stood near the window. The market reports came in from the instrument, bellowed in a gruff voice. Miller worked the dial. There were snatches of song, jazz orchestra, and then again the market.

"Sometimes we get RKO on Fridays and they have an old fiddlers' concert. I ain't been able to get it lately. I guess they've cut 'em out. Nobody cares much for that kind of music anymore."

Mrs. Miller came to the door.

"Dinner's ready," she called.

The two men arose. As they walked into the dining room Miller said, "By the way, Mr. Groves, if you want that instrument that . . . what d'ye call it, take it along with you out to California. It's no good here."

Old Roscoe paused beside his chair and looked out the window across the stubble field toward the river. Then slowly he said, "Oh, I guess I won't bother. I guess no one cares for them old things any more. The probably wouldn't even know what it was. It's been a long time since them was used at dances. They dance different now, too. Yes. Everything's different."

"Sit right down, Mr. Groves."

The tiny blond child came shyly into the room. Her mother seated her across from old Roscoe. She looked at him curiously. Suddenly she broke into a prolonged giggle.

"Shhh!" said her mother as the child hid her face in her napkin. "Don't act that way."

The child gave another little suppressed giggle, looked again at old Roscoe, and turned to her mother while the perspiring woman tucked a white napkin under her daughter's chin.

Old Aches and Bloody Claws

Looking across the Wapsipinicon from the stone steps in front of the grocery store in Ontarns, Old Dick could see for the first time in that early spring season the dancing heat waves as they vibrated over the hillside above the cedar-fretted limestone bluff. Tomorrow he'd probably see a bluebird. In a few days someone would tell him on these same stone steps that they had heard the piping of frogs in some pasture pond. And then it would not be long before there would be talk of planting corn because "the burroak leaves are as big as a squirrel's ear."

Winter seems long to those who wait for seed time and old joints ache after a winter of damp, so Old Dick was the first man to sit down beside Turner, the groceryman, on the stone steps in the sun.

"Well, how are you, Dick?" asked Turner, as he lighted his stump of cigar, and switched it about in his mouth.

The large, gaunt old man spat out a huge cud of tobacco over his silver beard and took his time answering. At last, he said, "Good, if it wasn't for this damned rheumatism."

"Think a storm's brewin'?" asked Turner.

A man with a sooty smudge of a blacksmith shop joined the men and seated himself beside Old Dick.

"What's that you say about rheumatism, Dick?" he asked as he filled his pipe from a greasy pouch.

"Oh, I was just tellin' Turner it's about got me down."

A battered Ford stopped at the store and a young farmer with a case of eggs came up.

"Hello, Fred," Turner, the groceryman, half-grunted.

The young farmer placed his egg-case near the door, taking a seat near Turner.

"A man ain't got no business to put up with rheumatism," said the blacksmith as he blew out a great cloud of smoke.

"What the hell you goin' to do about it, then?" bellowed the old man.

"There's no use tryin' to tell you. You'd just make fun of it," said the blacksmith.

"No, I wouldn't," groaned the old man. "I've got to the point where I'd try anything."

From across the street came the town barber, a cigarette dangling from the corner of his mouth, the sun shining through his green eye shade and his soiled white jacket flapping about his lean frame. He stood near the door of the store with his hands in his trousers pockets.

Old Dick finished stuffing a handful of cigar clippings into his mouth.

"Well, what's your cure?" he roared.

"The blacksmith reached into his pocket and rummaged around. The men grouped around him.

"There," he said with a note of triumph, "is the thing that cured me."

"Buckeyes?" queried the barber.

"Call 'em that if you want to. Some do, but the right name for 'em is horse chestnuts."

The young farmer laughed boisterously.

"There's a tree of 'em on our place, Dick. Come down and you can have all you want."

The farmer laughed again.

Old Dick took two of the objects in his hand and examined them closely. His face wore an incredulous expression.

"Hell!" he muttered. "How could them things help rheumatism?" He handed them back to the blacksmith.

"I won't answer you," growled the blacksmith. "I knowed you'd sneer at 'em."

"I wish to God I could get one of them rheumatism rings they sold at that Indian medicine show here a few years ago," Old Dick said mournfully. "Them was the only things ever helped me."

The blacksmith sniffed.

"What was in them rings do you s'pose?" asked Turner, the groceryman.

"I don't know," replied Old Dick, "but it was some sort of a composition of metals that generated electricity when it was against the heat of your hand. They done the business. I lost mine and never got a chance to get another one."

"They say that if a feller puts his hand in a swarm of bees and lets 'em sting him it'll cure rheumatiz," said the barber.

A roar of laughter greeted this and the barber's sallow face showed color as he nervously lighted another cigarette.

"I'd as soon have the rheumatiz as be stung by a mess of bees," said Turner.

"By God, I don't know about that," groaned Old Dick as he crossed his legs with difficulty.

The men looked across the river and silently watched the heat waves dance over the cornfield. The young farmer opened his mouth as though to speak and then smiled as he watched Old Dick, who was dreamily gazing up the river to where a limestone crag reflected the sun.

"Dick, what are you thinkin' about, lookin' up the river that way? Thinkin' about the time you caught the wildcat?"

A snicker from the blacksmith. Old Dick ground his quid.

"It'd be pretty hard to ketch a wildcat now with your rheumatism, wouldn't it, Dick?" asked Turner, grinning.

Old Dick waited. Then he spat on the stones and braced himself.

"Boys," he said, "it's nothin' to ketch a wildcat barehanded. I've done it time and again. They're scared when you get a bunch of dogs after 'em and get 'em treed. Of course there wa'n't any real good reason for me ketchin' 'em thataway, for I could always depend on the dogs. I had twenty hounds, you know. Good ones, too. Mostly blueticks and redbones I got from Kentucky. But the trouble was the dogs tore 'em up so. To save that, I got so every time I treed a bobcat I just climbed up the tree and nailed old mister cat—one hand on the nape of his neck and one on the small of his back and slid down with him. Wa'n't anything to it, and I saved the hounds from tearin' 'em to pieces. Anybody could do it if they just had the gall."

"God, I'd hate to try it," said Turner. His old Maltese cat had climbed up in his lap and was purring loudly as he stroked her back.

"Nothin' to it," answered Old Dick vigorously. "All you needed was gall and a good grip. Why, I remember once about forty years ago I got two big cats, a he and a she, one afternoon right on top of that big bluff up the river. The dogs had chased 'em all day, and about three o'clock they treed 'em in a big whiteoak there." He pointed with a long, gnarled finger.

The young farmer was grinning.

"I climbed up the tree with twenty feet of clothesline—cotton clothesline—wrapped around me. The dogs was so crazy that they knocked me down a half dozen times when I was tryin' to get up the tree. The he-cat was out on a limb. I edged up to him and grabbed him, as I've told you, by the back of the neck and the small of the back and pinned him there. Then I got him over against the trunk of the tree and tied him up. I done the same with the she-cat. By that time my father-in-law, who'd been huntin' with me, come along and beat the dogs back, so I could bring the cats down. I wanted to take 'em on the horse in front of my saddle and bring 'em down here, but I'd tied one of 'em so tight he was dead. The other one the old man made me turn loose so the dogs could kill. God, but there was a tussle!"

The barber began laughing a high falsetto laugh. A warning scowl from Turner made him stop.

"Of course you don't believe it," snapped Old Dick. "A white-livered devil like you who never seen a wildcat wouldn't believe it, of course! At that it wa'n't no great thing. Wildcats was timid things. All it took was a good grip and gall."

Two sparrows lighted on the flagstones in front of the store and began picking about among some crumbs. The old Maltese cat, which Turner held on his lap, ceased purring and straightened up with an eye on the birds. Turner grinned at the young farmer and pointed at the cat.

Old Dick had tossed his great quid away and was stuffing his pipe with tobacco.

"There's no wildcats around here now is there, Dick?" asked the blacksmith.

"None for thirty year," answered Old Dick. I killed the last pair about that long ago, just before I went to Missouri. I shot one when the dogs treed him, and the dogs killed the other one. I shook him out of a saplin' and they finished him. I always felt a little mean over that. I didn't give him no chance. That was the same year that I had all the fun with the peddler that come to my house. I've told you about that."

"No, I don't remember," said the blacksmith.

"Well, a Jew peddler came to our house one evening about supper time and wanted to stay all night. We didn't want to bother with him, but I couldn't get shet of him. After supper I set smokin' and got to tellin' him about wildcats. I could see he was scared stiff. Then I went upstairs and brought down the sack of six wildcat skins I had. I spread 'em all out on the floor. 'Where did you kill 'em,' the little Jew asked, with his eyes poppin' out of his head. 'Oh, right back of the house,' I says. Then I says, 'I've got to go down to the barn.' When I got back, the Jew peddler was gone and I could see him about a mile down the road with his pack on his back, makin' tracks."

The laughter that followed was suddenly interrupted. Another sparrow had joined the two on the flagstones and the temptation was more than Turner's old Maltese cat could resist. Old Dick had bent down to strike a match on a flagstone, and just as he straightened up, the cat made a spring for the sparrows. Old Dick was sitting just below Turner, and as he sat up again, he was directly in the cat's way. The creature struck Old Dick squarely on the shoulders, and finding its progress impeded, began to claw at the denim jacket, furiously attempting to free itself of the thing which had blocked its way.

There then went up howls of laughter from the corded throats of spectators. John Rohn, the groceryman across the street, saw the cat clawing Old Dick's back and yelled encouragement. Dick sprang to his feet, a look of genuine terror on his sallow, old, wind-lashed face. When he saw the Maltese cat scurrying through the door of the grocery, his expression changed. The spectators laughed uproariously but began to quiet down when they saw Old Dick's face. Angry, they knew how he could blast one with his whiplash tongue, but now they saw that the look on Old Dick's face was not one of anger, but the half-ashamed, half-sorrowful look of impotency which come at times to the old when they suddenly discover themselves beaten by some weak thing of which yesterday they were master.

Old Dick straightened his shabby black hat and looked across the street toward where two men were pitching horseshoes.

"I guess I'll go over and pitch a game or two myself," he muttered. Then he limped away, the men's eyes following him. Turner dusted off his knees and stood up. The blacksmith likewise. Turner took the handle of the egg-case and started through the door. The young farmer followed.

"Old Dick couldn't wrassle a field mouse now with that rheumatiz of his," said the barber to the blacksmith as they crossed the street.

"No, but I believe he'd get over it if he'd only do what I told him to, but he's so damn set."

"Yes, and then his age is agin' him," said the barber as he turned and went down the sidewalk toward the place where Old Dick was scrutinizing a pair of polished horseshoes with the eye of one who loves good tools and the feel of them.

II.
Poetry

Birds of Prey

I saw an osprey
Soaring in the heavens,
Floating high on strong pinions,
Monarch of all beneath him.
He sailed and wheeled over a lake,
Pausing a moment: then, arrow-like,
He struck the cool water with a splash,
Emerging with a wriggling fish
Firmly grasped in his talons.

Another day I watched him
Leave the huge oak
Where his mate mothered two fledglings.
Scarce was he well on his way
When two smaller birds pursued him—
Two tiny kingbirds—mere specks,
But I could hear their screeching
As they rushed their giant quarry.
They worried and harassed him
Until he took refuge in the forest depths,
Helpless against the fury of their assaults.

Yesterday I visited a courtroom.
There I listened to the trial of a man.
Once he had been a power in the world of finance.
There were the judge and the bailiff
And the men of law,
Mighty in their little places.

I heard him tell the faltering story of his misdeeds,
And then his attorney pleaded for him.
I gazed about on the curious crowd
That had gathered to see a man fight for his future—
Morbid women, idle men, streetwalkers.
Some grinned and gaped, some whispered,
Some wiped their necks with grimy handkerchiefs,
Some shuffled their feet, some chewed gum.
To them it was not a tragic struggle—
It was an entertainment
Which they welcomed and entered into greedily.

And I minded me of the great osprey,
That mighty bird of prey
Helpless and hemmed in by his little adversaries.

A White Pigeon

What bizarre whim
Of Fate
Has cast you
Into this maelstrom
Called a city?

You...
The symbol of peace,
Gentle bearer of the olive branch,
Emblem of quiet purity...
Your soiled feathers
Represent grimmest irony...
The irony
Of living.

A girl
Watches you with sad eyes,
As you trail in the gutter
For scraps of food.

Is it, perchance,
That in her heart
She understands you?
You...
Whom the city has also stained
With its grime.

THE FOLK DANCER

I watched you dance;
Your graceful limbs
Were quartz crystals,
Sparkling,
Iridescent,
Refracting the light
Into all the splendid colors
Of the spectrum.

Your swaying body
Moved like a rhythm
Of a poem.

A fairy wand
Seemed to touch me.
I grew young . . .
Watching you dance.

EGO

A field mouse
Doubtless thinks
That the farmer
Places corn shocks
For its shelter.

"Here comes my supper!"
Said the weasel,
Speaking of
This same mouse.

"How fortunate,"
Says the society belle,
"That there are weasels
To provide me
With imitation ermine!"

"I am glad
That this great tree
Was put here
As a location for my nest!"
Cried the magpie.

"How kind of someone
To make this ocean
For me to swim in!"
Quoth the herring.

Don't pity the savage
Because he is naked.
He is sorry for us
Because we must wear clothes.

"Look,"
Says the proud mother,
"They're all out of step
But my Jim!"

The pronoun "I"
Is very frail,
Because worn thin
By constant use.

Often I think
Everybody's queer . . .
But me.

THE CARDINAL

To him
Of the understanding heart,
Each day
Hath its lesson. . . .

I have found
My lesson for today. . . .
My tutor
Was a scarlet cardinal,
Who darted like a tongue of flame
Among the bare elm branches.

I,
Deep in selfish thought,
Stood watching the east
Tint like a conch shell . . .
When suddenly
Up spoke my red-garbed preceptor:
"What cheer?"

Ah,
What a divine question
For the waking earth to answer,
Morning by morning!

But earth
Would have to be ready
With an answer,
Even as I have resolved
To be ready with my answer,
And it must be full
Of joy and thankfulness:
But principally . . .
Joy.

"What cheer?"
Ah, crested cardinal,
That is all there is
To life, after all, isn't it? . . .
Cheer!
Are you listening there,
Gray world? . . .
"What cheer?"

THE ETCHER

Dear,
Time is an etcher,
Who scratches fine, fine lines
In your face . . .
To tell their little story
Of joy and grief,
Love and disappointment.
But, as Time works,
It seems to me
You grow only more lovely!

Dear,
Time is an etcher . . .
But, in his wisdom,
He makes
Trees and mountains and faces
Always and only
More beautiful.

THE MINISTER'S WIFE

Ours is a peaceful town
Of a thousand souls or so.
It is cradled among the hills,
And we are provincial,
Self-satisfied,
And contented. . . .
But souls must be saved,
So we hire parsons to do this
Little service for us,
And we have five churches
Whose lofty spires,
Like great inverted icicles,
Pierce the blue sky
Overhead.

No, I shall not waste time
Telling you of the five pastors
Who labor in those churches—
Though many noble things might be said of them
And the good works wrought by their hands.

Nay,
I have rather to speak of a woman
Whom I saw today. . . .
She stood in a doorway
Of a modest cottage,
Watching her three children
As they left for school.

Her calico dress was a little faded,
And her smile a little tired
And worried.
Her face was pinched
And wore the gray shadow of self-denial,
But she waved a joyous goodbye
To the neatly-dressed children.

I have seen her frequently before,
In various places.
I have seen her in church,
In her run-over shoes and shabby hat,
For she teaches a Sunday School class.
I have seen her calling on the sick.
I have heard the kind words she spoke to a shiftless loafer.
I have seen the warming smile she gave a wayward girl....
The village Magdalene.
I have heard her voice in the choir,
Singing old hymns....

But once I saw a flush creep over her face,
And her eyes flashed fire.
That was when the banker's pretty daughter
Tittered at her old-fashioned coat....
But this was the only sign
That jibes stung her,
Or that her cross was heavy....
She is a brave woman.

In our village,
Souls must be saved.
And souls may be the property
Of humans exceeding poor in purse.
And ministers have wives ...
And oh,
We expect so much of them!
Poor things!
Why do we watch them so closely,
Expecting them to set an example
For us—
Who have less privation
And so little that calls
For rebellion?

CROWS

A swaying black procession
    From wooded copse and plain,
    Is moving to the tinted west,
    As even' comes again.

Their silence is uncanny.
    This somber raven crowd
Seems strangely stricken, half afraid
    To cry their woes aloud.

Voiceless till morn's red breaking,
    Silent their rasping call . . .
Do crows, like men, have solemn thoughts
    When dusk begins to fall?

THE MYSTIC RIVER-POOL

The green heron,
    silent,
    moping on orange-colored stilts,
    knows much
    river-pool lore;
    he is my classmate.

He is possessed
    of infinite wisdom,
    and knows the mysterious secrets
    of all the tiny water folk.
Why do shells of crawfish
    redden among the rocks,
    while tracks of the ringtailed raccoon,
    like hieroglyphics,
    write epics in black ooze?
Where do the oval bluegill
    and the rune-shelled mussel
    spend their afternoons
    when yellow birch shadows
    darken the placid pool?

What of the little water spider
> (like some Ganges raftsman)
> with leaden eyes,
> and a body
> brown as rotting wood?
Sit and angle, yokel!
> doze under your straw thatch
> and drool over your pipestem,
> dreaming only of fish
> sizzling on red coals!
But the green heron and I
> will find content . . .
> large content . . .
> In the sweet silences,
> gathering endless lore
> of the tiny river folk.

My Neighbor

My neighbor's lawyer writes his will,
His parson bids him pray;
While I go humming lilting tunes
Or sing some frothy lay.

He stakes himself a churchyard lot,
And hoards up flakes of gold;
He asks me to remember I
Will soon be bent and old.

But still I search for orchid buds,
Weeds choke my maize and rye;
My neighbor sagely shakes his head
When he goes plodding by.

BEWILDERMENT

It appears that I face
An overwhelming dilemma:

Loquacious expounders
Of Asiatic legend
Thunder at me mightily
Of a certain fiery pit
Yawning hungrily
To receive me;
They suggest
There is one alternative
One only:
I may escape
By mingling
With them and their kind.

It puzzles me:
How choose
Between damnation and damnation?

RUBBISH

Today
I watched a toothless hag
Groping feverishly
With a hooked iron rod,
In the foul refuse
Of the city's dump.

Her frayed garments
And her sallow countenance
Harmonized weirdly
With her surroundings,
As the color of a worm
Matches old wood.

Her shriveled lips
Bore a cynical sneer,
Like the grin
Of a drying corpse.

And constantly she muttered
As she jabbed this way and that,
"Why is it . . .
Men always cast aside
That of which they tire?
While woman hide it
To cry over?"

TEMPTED

The tempter's voice
Is very insistent
Today.
I cannot help listening.
(And then, I want to listen!)
Shall I yet yield
To his pleadings?
My irreproachable family
(All of them deceased),
And my physician
(A most learned individual),
Together with my pastor
(A saintly scholar),
Have warned me often
Against most of the things
For which
I have felt any real attraction.
Until today,
I have dutifully heeded
Their admonitions.
But:
A week ago
My physician died,
Aged forty.
Yesterday
My pastor became involved
In a horrid scandal.
Today
I have a mind
To begin
To enjoy life!

THE WANDERER

A school of silver mackerel in the sky . . .
Gray oracles, bespeak tomorrow's rain.
On silken sails a sprite goes veering by—
A martin with his cloak of purple stain.
I hear the choir of the growing wheat,
And thrill in wonder at the bunting's note.
I listen with a sense of languor sweet,
To pulsings from the vireo's chaste throat.

They say I am a dreamer . . . and a throng
Are calling me an idler and a drone.
In vain I plead that I commit no wrong,
But only kneel before the soul's true throne.
I strive to show them beauty dwelling near—
How can a deaf-blind world presume to jeer?

SOULS

I am not anxious
Over the whereabouts
Of the souls of men and women,
Passed into some spaceless void
From the silent temples
Which were their clay abodes.

Laugh if you will . . .
But I have a strange notion
That yon clump of trees
Jutting the river
And crowning a rising hill,
Is a group of such souls
Come back to laugh
And sing and sigh.

See that gnarled oak:
I have a fancy
That is the soul
Of some village blacksmith.
Those knots on its trunk
Are like to hard lumps of muscle,
From daily pounding of steel
On iron anvils.

And that graceful sycamore,
Nude on the cliff,
Is it not a schoolboy
Poised for a dive
Into the river's clear depths?

That elm . . .
See how it stands
Proud of its chastity
Dignified and a little prudish?
Perhaps a teacher of children
In some narrow schoolroom.

I have virginal birches:
White birches . . .
Souls of nuns
Murmuring prayers.

When I have need
Of spiritual purging,
I shall mingle with trees,
Rather than with verbose bigots,
For I have a notion
That trees are souls
Pushing heavenward
From the sod.

FAILURES

Nearly the entire span
    of man's allotted
        three score and ten years
        has passed by him
        on review.

Penniless,
    a failure,
        this wrecked craft
        lies in a chaotic mass
        on life's reef—
        hull and spars
        shattered,
        broken,
        tangled . . .

Tell me
>how can he
>still smile?
>(Yet he does smile!)
>Let me point out to you
>>a marked contrast.
>Yonder goes the president
>>of our largest bank.
>He is rated at two million!
>There is success for you!
>There is a man to pattern after!

What's that you say, newsboy?
"Horrible scandal?"
"Awful tragedy?"
"Millionaire banker accused by woman, suicides?"

Great god!
Banker Jones,
>right here in our own town!

See that old chap
>with his grandson,
>>digging fishworms?
He seems as happy
>as a king!

This very day
>I must look in my dictionary
>and strive to find the meaning
>of that word *failure*.

A GRAY-HAIRED BARD SPEAKS

I see you are amazed
That one with graying locks,
Should touch a golden lute
Adore the rose and phlox—
Delight in lays of birds,
And toy with silver words!

But these gray strands I wear
Speak of another day
When I let grief walk in
And drive my song away.
Now have I banished care
Therefore my song is fair!

I treasure deep those scars—
And I must not forget.
Yea, every gash and mark
I'll keep and cherish—yet
My heart must be a lark
To trill before the dark!

GENUS HOMO

Man will worship beauty
On his bended knees;
Then with plowshare and ax blade
Blot out grass and trees.

Great love for his brother,
Loudly he proclaims,
And yet this selfsame brother
He murders and maims.

When he sees a neighbor
Stumble on life's road,
How swift he rushes past him
With his own light load!

And he struts with ego
In the sun's white rays;
While alone in the black night
He trembles and prays.

TO A FISH HAWK

Ah! You've returned once more
To that cedar on the cliff;
You watch again with cynical eyes
The fisherman row his skiff.

Stop! Don't spread frightened wings
For I know an osprey's soul.
Perhaps I once smote a river's breast
Or veered thru the sky's curved bowl.

Stay! Was I once a hawk
Or will I be one that day
My soul shall cast off its bands of steel
And start to flutter away?

Oh! You have left me here,
Feet gripped by this quicksand bar.
You'll go your way ere night spreads its crepe—
I'll sink while watching a star.

OPEN SEASON

Above me sounded notes from whirring wings:
    I looked—and there, sharp-etched against the sky,
There sped upon the gale two lovely things,
    A brace of teal—they made me yearn to fly!
I little dreamed that fiends with tools of death
    Were ambushed in a willow clump close by.

A barrel vomits flame—a pinion fails;
    Grey breath of powder weaves a curling frieze.
Another belch of Hell leaves ashen veils,
    While voice of thunder whips the fretful breeze!
When nightfall swathed the bayou in its crepe,
There came a sound like sobbing from the trees.

A MAIZE COUNTRY PIONEER'S INTERMENT

The hired man has donned his Sunday suit.
He wears, as well, his most effusive air.
His badge of mourning is a larded boot—
A slouch hat wreathed in crepe—well-plastered hair;
A collar that is slashing at his jowls,
A figured waistcoat—pale from age and wear.

The wheezy chug of motors down the lane
Bespeaks the coming of the farmer folk.
Some have remembered that his fields lay near.
They come to gaze upon this fallen oak,
Who, pale and rigored in his lacquered chest,
Sleeps, with his plow-worn palms across his breast.
There, in a vase close to his sunken cheek,
They have placed blossoms, bathed with dew this morn—
Flowers to him were weeds—did none bring corn—
One stalk of wheat—a wisp of bearded rye
Or anything which pleased his living eye?

Still these cracked hymn notes—let the soft voiced breeze
Sing this last dirge out in his maple trees!
If there be mourning, let the maize fields weep,
Before they lose him to this hillside sleep!

What shall the cassocked one say of this man?
He never crossed a cloistered church's sill,
Yet find for me in all this countryside
One who will breathe of him a word of ill!

Hear how the parson gropes—and tries to spin
Words—here's a problem for this man of God.
How shall he list such breakers of the sod
Who scorn to kneel and pray, yet never sin?

It is not long—this last ride that he takes.
Only two miles—yet never in his day
Did he go down this road with neighbor folk
Following close and weeping on the way.
This is a time his virtues fill their thoughts,
Now they are troubled that he could not stay.

The timbered hillock waits—its granite shafts
Seem to be groomed in honor of a guest.
There is one spot where earth reveals a scar,
But this is sutured soon . . . the last spade pressed.
Earth takes him back again—then cloaks her breast.

God or the devil cares not for his husk,
But one of them, ere now, possesses his soul.
Maggots are greedy worms—flesh is their goal.
And when they've left him tombed within that hill,
His children hasten home to scan his will.

MAIZE COUNTRY NATAL DAY

The doctor rubs his heavy-lidded eyes
And takes his shaggy fur coat from a chair.
Above the woodlot knoll the last star dies,
A cock's first metal call rides on the air.
The midwife tiptoes down the creaking stair—
New day finds voice in raucous barnyard cries.

The littered bedroom now is hushed and chill
And underneath a soiled and tattered quilt
Which swathes the pain-racked figure on the bed
A new life starts its gropings in a world
That metes out crumbs of joy—much toil—some bread
And gives a turf-locked lodging to its dead.

Now comes a thin cry from the ragged cot:
The flame of mother love has come to stay
Within a heart which knows so much of hurt—
So much of yearnings, choked and put away:
Her wan breasts now must fill to nurture life;
This is one mission of a prairie wife!

Out in the stable by dim lantern light,
The drowsy farmer hears the rhythmic tone
Of pearl white milk streams on his bucket's tin:
The hungry horses neigh and stamp—the groan
Of soft-eyed cows seems like a milk protest,
Because a mouth was added to that brood
Demanding that their udder yield more food!

The collie yelps and scratches at the door
Or vents in barks his bitter, pent up spleen.
His canine instinct seeming to convey
The message that his girth must now grow lean
Henceforth will cast off bones be nibbled clean!

The squealing swine within their filthy sty
Are chafing with their hunger at the trough.
The hills look down in silence and the rows
Of corn stalks march in lines and taper off
Beyond the hilltop where the stubble land
Awaits the plowshare and a steady hand.
Hunger and still more hunger clamors loud,
Waiting the filling bulk of maize and wheat—
Seeming to cry: "Oh, bring us loaves and meat!"
And, to combat this hunger of old Earth,
Women must groan in travail, giving life
That these wide fields may know the hoe and plow:
This is one mission of a prairie wife.

FORECAST

The drumsticks of a storm tonight will beat
Upon my roof a martial roundelay.
I know—for mares' tails in the blue are flung,
And mackerel swim there . . . foam-flecked and grey.

I watched brown spiders reinforce their webs;
An old wife placed a barrel 'neath the eaves:
My windmill's wheel was fretful thru the day—
While maples showed the lining of their leaves.

And when the pearl grey beast of morrow's dawn
Shall press once more against night's murky stain,
My sleep-locked lids shall open but to close—
Sealed by the deft witch-fingers of the rain!

PASTORAL

Are you that same one
Who but yesteryear
Made the cheeks of yokel swain
Tint when you came near?

I saw your photo
In your nuptial veil,
With your chaste nun's countenance—
Mask-like and pale.

Now you're a slattern
In your hillside nest,
With your offspring tugging at
Your loose, shapeless breast!

Why does a woman
Soon grey like a clod,
When she is bound through wedlock
To the loam and sod?

A PLOWMAN SINGS

My plowshare sheds its winter coat of rust
And cuts a channel thru earth's loamy crust.

My panting span plod on with sweaty coats—
Their trace-chains marking time with metal notes.

A grackle in my furrow flutters down,
Resplendent in his purple velvet gown.

While clods are falling from my moldboard's keel,
Wee field folk feel the vengeance of its steel.

The meadow mouse in terror leaves her nest.
There is a panic in the gopher's breast.

A lizard's slimy form is cut in twain,
The horned lark seeks her cup-shaped home in vain.

That drunken god of lightning whips a cloud
And bellows at the hilltops, long and loud.

His curses dying in a groan of pain—
He whispers husky promises of rain.

My neighbor waves a greeting from his hill
And motions to the storm clouds' sooty frill.

I know that he is laughing as he goes,
Because I'm still at plowing, while he sows!

He fails to understand how I can sing,
Holding no grudge against a tardy spring.

And later on when summer rules the sky,
He'll point to mustard in my oats and rye.

He guesses not, that as I plod along,
My heart's a seedbed for a crop of song!

Autumn Nocturne—Maize Village Grocery Store

They come to intermingle—kindred souls—
Philosopher, grey seer and youthful wit.
The cordwood chunk within the iron stove
Has loosed its heat—the spooky shadows flit
And make grotesque these sagging, gabbling mouths,
Adrip with curses and tobacco spit.

One has a visage like some bird of prey—
A hawk's face—where an ugly leer has set.
One has the beard and eyebrows of a faun—
One wears the features of a marmoset.
One sits apart like some fat Rabelais,
Releasing guffaws when a jibe is met.

They are concerned with neighbors' barns and flocks.
They talk of amours of the hillside folk.
They fling barbed word-shafts at the landed rich
Or hypocrite who hides beneath a cloak.
They pass harsh sentence on all scheming ones
Who seek to load their shoulders with a yoke.

The yellow maize is ripe and garnered in.
Another coat of rust is on their plows.
Another winter's snow must shroud their fields
Before the pale leaves on the burroak boughs
Will bid these tired grubbers seek the soil
To plant again a crop for swine and cows.

Ever it was since man has tilled the earth.
He must have laughter, gossip, spans of rest.
After the harvest when his bins are full
He craves to hear his fellows boast and jest.
Man, though a creature of the clods and loam,
Harbors a throbbing thing within his breast.

Retired

He has sprung from the loins of one who found
A path across a chartless span of plain.
And he was nurtured at a mother's breast
Who, wanting little, toiled with rough, red hands
And took a wage of crusts and childbirth pain.

His eyes first opened on an unplowed world
Where life was only for the sinewed few.
Pied tiger lilies, in that grassy maze,
Gave him a welcome from their ragged stems—
Standing on guard beneath a tent of blue.

His bare feet came to know the furrow soon,
And soon his palms were curved to grasp a hoe.
His ear was tuned to catch the cock's first call—
His back was corded well that it might bend
To move along above a weedy row.

Choosing a mate, he sought no comely form,
But looked for one to sweep his kitchen floor.
He wanted one with hands to knead coarse bread—
One with firm knees to grip a milk-pail's flanks
And strength to carry water to his door.

Now his broad acres spread and ripple off,
Marked by the lines of marching corn and cane.
Great barns are hunched above his mounds of hay—
Fat cattle stand and low at feeding time—
His hills are greening from their gifts of rain.

But he is gone and some drab village street
Each day is conscious of his restless tread.
Mutely he plods throughout his taskless day
Or sits beside his somber, toothless mate,
Letting time glide above his weathered head.

There is a strange hand on his stable's latch—
There is an alien voice to call his sheep—
More pliant fingers shape his shocks of oats,
His horses neigh and wait for him in vain,
The loam is ready for his time of sleep.

Visitor

I knew he held the tang of stack and mow—
    One sensed that he was brother to the soil.
    His palms were stained with signs of stable toil
And calloused by the handles of his plough.

Yet I felt closely bound to him by ties—
    I knew the countryside where he was born.
    I'd seen its hillsides green with rows of corn,
And now I saw its meadows in his eyes.

For he had kept deep-rooted in the clay
    While I had chosen marketplace and street.
    I knew the city's bricks would bruise his feet
And send him soon to go his plodding way.

But he had sought me out to grip my hand
    And sit for one short hour by my chair.
    Our talk was of the things that happen where
The souls of men have kinship with the land.

I asked him of the orchard and the grove,
    About the bayou with its reedy shore,
    About the grey one in the village store
Who used to doze beside a ruddy stove.

He told me how the creek had changed its bed,
    And how his acres spread across the hill.
    The hours wore and he was talking still,
And I was hungry for the things he said.

Then I who long had pitied peasant folk
    And broken faith with field and pasture ground
    Felt dull and leaden-footed in my round
And strangely like a cart-beast with a yoke.

Surcease

Now comes a little span when farmers rest
    Before the new corn shows each pale, green hill—
Before the rank weeds anchor choking roots
    And fling their poison shade to blight and kill.

And horses, out to pasture on a knoll
    Show broad, white bands across their shoulders now,
Where sweat and froth beneath each harness trap
    Gathered like seafoam as they dragged the plow.

The wood thrush sees that work is laid aside
    And calls forth preludes from his golden horn,
Knowing that man deserves a taste of joy
    For routing hunger with a crop of corn.

Hill Soul's Death

She passed along a little span of life
    When beauty held her close—but not for long
Did she keep a soul which thrilled to stirring things,
    Like suns behind a bank of a veery's song.

So soon the very loam through which she walked,
    Clogging her footsteps, made of her a serf
Like her neighbors with their loose and sagging breasts
    And their hopes that never rose above the turf.

And the pulse which beat in rhythm through her wrists
    When a hill swain blushed and stammered awkward vows,
Has no more urge to set it throbbing now
    But is locked like sap in winter maple boughs.

Prairie Bachelor

His fields are wide and furrowed well in spring.
    He fills great bins with wheat—his stacks are tall.
His shoats and lambs are fat for slaughtering.
    Great apple trees drop crimson globes in fall—
Strutting about his bulging, painted barns
    Are silken-feathered cocks that send their call
And greet the sunrise with a beating wing.

Yet, when his toil-wrapped form is gripped by sleep,
    A phantom woman stands beside his bed.
She brings a gift his eager soul would keep—
    She shapes a dream to dance within his head.
When he awakes to find that she is gone,
    He waits for dawn to stain the skyline red,
Staring in space with eyes that dare not weep.

Grubber's Day

Morning came up as other mornings came:
    A paling star above his woodlot hill—
A score of lean swine clamoring for swill.
    His woman there to start the cookstove's flame.

He lit his lantern and its rays were dim.
    The sting was in his loins for night had kept
Him grubbing in his dreams while he had slept—
    Stiffness and furrow-ache were kin to him.

The draft horse in the stall gave out a neigh—
    Sensing the man's approach—a brother beast
Yet happier with his proffered morning feast
    Than he who filled the manger full of hay.

The milch cows in their stanchions saw him quaff
    A dram of harsh new brandy from a tin.
They lowed and grudged their master this small sin,
    And nuzzled in the fodder rack for chaff.

After the bleating ewes and lambs were fed,
    He treaded up the path—the kitchen smells
Were like the subtle things with lead to hells
    By promising a respite on ahead.

Across the table sat the shrunken husk
    Which mated with his body and his soil
And likewise took, a few crusts for her toil
    Plodding her kitchen rounds from dawn to dusk.

After the scalding morning sun was hung,
    He curved his calloused palms about a rein
And plodded down a slope, then back again
    With groans and muttered curses on his tongue.

Even the hawk and rabbit left his fields.
    Only the turkey vulture kept the sky.
The mouse and bug forsook his plot of rye,
    Searching for fertile loam with better yields.

No hint of wild rose on his rutted slope—
    No stray flint arrowhead upon the sand,
No spikenard for the blister on his hand,
    And not a lark to sound a note of hope.

When shadows on the hillside pointed noon
    His horses turned their hooves—he trailed behind.
Then at his frugal board again to find
    The same plate with his cup and battered spoon.

Returning to his square of land once more,
    He found the sun had strengthened and the dust
Came in his face with every passing gust—
    He found the corn rows longer than before.

The only sound the afternoon could give
    Was croaking from the crows which stole his seed.
He wondered if the birds had known his need
    Leaving in pity some that he might live.

Dusk was the same as morning; then his frame
    Found half oblivion, the gift of night.
One day—a tiny fragment of a fight
    With hill clay always victor in the game.

LANDLOCKED SAILOR

No other man along the ridge
Could splice a hay rope's strands,
And he had queer, blue anchor things
Tattooed upon his hands.

He swore the sort of heavy oaths
Which only seamen swear.
His clumsy footgear was the kind
Which old salt sailors wear.

Rough days he'd ask, "How would ye like
To climb a mast today?
Fer she'll be choppier than Hell
And soak the deck with spray!"

At other times he'd sit and dream
While rainbows curved their stripes.
Some brighter days he'd whistle tunes
Filled with the lilt of pipes.

I've seen him let his hay be wet
While whittling out the prows
Of tiny, masted, sailing boats,
Or larger fishing scows.

But on day when a windstorm broke
I saw him almost cry,
Because two lost, bewildered gulls
Went veering through the sky.

TAXIDERMIST

To him it was a tragic thing
For mole or grouse or brant to die
And all the husks of slaughtered teal
He wanted kept close by.

He seemed to think the souls of quail
Would flutter back to mounted skins
And by his strange and savage rites
Be purged of birdly sins.

And in his smelly, cobwebbed shop
He loved to sit when twilight fell
And for the ones who spoke his tongue,
Strange tales he used to tell.

The language that his soul preferred
In street or in his bartering
Was much the same the grocer used
When tying ends of string.

But when he put his scalpel up
And hung his apron by the stove
His talks were of the rail and tern
That haunt the marshy cove.

His mates were sunburned, hawk-eyed men
Who seldom worked and always owed—
Men who lived near heron roosts
Along the river road.

To a Wounded Mallard in Midwinter

It takes a weary span of days
To mend a buckshot shattered wing
And a prairie marsh, ice-locked and dead,
Where a buzzard poises overhead
Invites no bird to wait for spring.

You came down with the equinox
Searching for slugs and buried seeds
But your mates went on like arrow shafts
While you and two dead feathered rafts
Went drifting windward through the reeds.

Stay on here in my pasture lot—
My gun is red with winter rust.
The creek that gives my draught-team drink
Has open pools and a cress-fringed brink,
And none comes here you cannot trust.

Preen your quills while the snow god raves—
Spring will waken some wild mate's cry.
I'll set strong traps when the bayou thaws
For any mink with unfriendly claws
And woe to the hawk that haunts this sky!

Hooked Rug

The attic gave its share—
Each raveled, faded shred
Which long had mildewed there
Held kinship with the dead.

This coat a fighter had
Before his lips went mute.
It made a ridge road lad
March proudly to a flute.

This crinoline and lace,
All ribbon-decked and pale
Was worn beneath a face
That later knew a veil.

This spangled crimson frock
Which harbors wasp and mouse
Beneath that broken clock,
Has known a gayer house.

Oh, do not pry too deep
Among these buried things!
Oh, let the dead past keep
These letters bound by strings!

Handcraft may weave red birds
From garret-gathered cloth,
But leave the warp of words
To feed some silent moth!

RIDGE ROAD WIFE'S HOLIDAY

They threshed the crop of clover seed,
    The oats and rye were in the bin—
The corn was ripe and clean from weed,
    The apples had been gathered in.

And then there came a rainy span,
    Too wet for labor in the field.
What better time to coax a man
    Than when the corn rows hold a yield?

The wagon crawled—they took their way
    Which passed the sumac-covered knoll;
What matter if the fog was gray
    When there was singing in the soul?

What matter, if when night goes black
    She's weary at her kitchen rounds?
She has a new shawl for her back
    And in her ears are city sounds!

The Younger Ridge Road Men

The younger ridge road men have lost
    The skill to make a helve or yoke.
They cannot tell the older tales
    That have delighted older folk.

They know the haunt of fox and mink
    But do not know the bait to use,
And few of them when autumn comes
    Would know the size of trap to choose.

At night around the ruddy stove
    They listen to the blacksmith tell
Of his philandering and fights,
    Of how he welds an axle well.

They hear of how their fathers cursed
    And how their grandsires leveled elms,
Of how they came from other shores
    In ships with tempest-battled helms.

But younger ridge road men will smile,
    Then tap their foreheads . . . jibe and grin
And veer the stove-side talk around
    To later styles of toil and sin.

The grizzled ridge road men agree
    The younger ones are soft these days.
They cannot hew a helve or yoke—
    They even sin the softer ways.

Hill Spinster's Sunday

Some subtle alchemy within her flesh
    Aroused an old, chained song and set it free.
It stilled a moment, mounting up afresh—
    The high, cracked voices droned in dreary key.

Surcease from toil was hers today, she knew.
    The hills were blizzard-bound . . . the fields were white:
No beets to weed; no kitchen work to do,
    And all her fires banked to challenge the night.

An afternoon of sensuous dreams begun—
    A tiny span of secret warming sin:
A strange, platonic orgy, swiftly done,
    But cherished well and safely locked within.

The rolling organ notes are silent soon—
    The road is long before she finds her bed:
So stumbling on beneath a grinning moon,
    She goes without the Christ she ached to wed.

LOAM-WOUNDED

Indian Summer suns may blaze a trail
Over the smoky sky before the dusk.
The days are all alike as huddled quail—
The ripened corn is waiting in the husk.

Last year—the year before—a dozen falls
He was the first to fill his crib to roof.
But now the cock each morning wastes his calls
His hungry broodmare paws with restless hoof.

The ghosts of other harvests fill his dreams—
At noon he looks for her about the stove.
He starts when owls greet starlight with their screams—
And thinks he sees strange prowlers in his grove.

She bore the years and kept a little song.
The hatching seasons—haying times—ripe fruit,
These came but, as the twelve months trooped along,
Her voice found shrill, queer trebles like a flute.

She used to watch him on that wheatfield knoll,
And when she drove his sweaty plow-span in,
She tried to reach some softness in his soul
By talking of his fanning mill and bin.

Drab weeks of emptiness kept dragging past
Until the lay she crooned was but a wail.
They put her with the mumbling ones at last
And left him mateless, chained to scythe and flail.

He gropes for her at midnight in his bed
Then takes his flask in palsied, barn-stained hands.
His hungry swine are squealing to be fed—
The smartweeds spill their black seed on his lands.

His kitchen holds the hush of dead men's halls;
And morning finds his earthen jug well-drained,
But through the copper coils within his walls
All night the drops of dream-stuff softly rained.

He finishes his harvesting when snow
Has threatened long to bury deep his crop.
The woman in her prison mutters low
But gnawing mice will hear his vintage drop.

The woman in that cell will fall to dust—
The man who digs these slopes forsake his toil—
But still there come new lines of blood which must
Wage on this futile fight with rutted soil.

Second Marriage

He cut a bee tree when the linden leaves
    Held still the green of summer in their veins.
In spite of rust, good rye was in his sheaves—
    He finished threshing long before the rains.

He had a cask with purple, wild grape wine;
    He had a heifer, fat for slaughtering—
The last few melons ripened on his vine;
    There was enough of wood to last till spring.

His daughter had been wedded to the one
    Who owned the fertile acres on the knoll.
He heard the best of tidings from his son,
    And winter found him glad within his soul.

Seldom had any season been so filled—
    He whistled at his evening choring rounds;
Fruit in his orchard . . . ample flour milled—
    Rabbits abundant . . . two young beagle hounds.

His mate was bent and silent, but he knew
    She plied a busy needle, and her bread
Was light . . . her kitchen tasks were never through,
    And every noontime saw her table spread.

She had no knack for love-craft, nor had he.
    Their talk was always talk of corn or hives;
Talk of the neighbor's barns, which they could see—
    Talk of the simple things which touched their lives.

How they had joined in flesh, I never knew—
    They seemed two dull, clay puppets, and the sod
Seemed like an earthy setting for these two
    Who moved and bred to please some drunken god.

But this warm, pulsing one he later gave
    The place within his kitchen—was she wooed
After the grass had found the other's grave
    Or did she trade her body for his food?

Did she make swift appraisal of his lands
    Or has she pity, buried out of sight?
Fancy a soft embrace from his rough hands
    And picture him upon his bridal night!

Theirs must have been a courtship, strange indeed!
    His woman died in March, and from that day,
He tramped his muddy oatfield with his seed—
    Weeping and cursing in a wild, mad way.

Telling the people who would pass him by,
    What he had lost, and how he hated life.
Some folks may understand it, but not I,
    For Autumn found him with this other wife!

Scant signs of wooing . . . but we saw him go
    On Sundays to the church with shaven chin,
Driving his span along the willow row—
    The same thin team which brought his fodder in.

How did he put his peasant grief aside? . . .
    What does a tired hillside grubber know
Of women, of a bridal night or bride
    When all he ever did was plow and sow?

But here she is: a younger, singing wife,
    Stirring his steaming porridge after dusk.
Will next year's harvest find her giving life—
    This fresh, strange creature, tethered to a husk?

She is not deaf . . . she listens to him now—
    Listens to stove-side talk of fields and seed,
Of ewes and harrows . . . clover in the mow—
    Theirs must have been a courtship strange indeed.

SOLILOQUY ON A RIVER ROAD

I took the longer way across the swale.
    I took this rougher way to miss the sight
Of tombstones in the sunlight, cold and pale
    And specter-like and white.

I passed the place that had the sagging fence;
    The house that had the shattered windowpanes—
The yard was clogged with horseweeds, foul and dense,
    The pastures gashed from the rains.

I know the tenant of this somber place,
    I often see him in his rutted fields.
I know the signs upon his worried face
    Deep etched from year on year of scanty yields.

I know the dozen others of his kind
    That live along this stony river road.
I know the barrenness of every mind—
    I know their debtor's load.

And yet I go his way to miss the signs
    Of struggles given up, those marble things—
Those live-forever plants, those tangled vines—
    The graven names and carven angel wings.

I know the ones beneath those grassy mounds
    Are sightless to the flight of brant and teal;
Are deaf to all the friendly river sounds—
    They lie in loam they cannot feel.

These other ones may roundly curse the soil,
    May lash their plodding, balky, bony teams,
But they at least can plan a crop and toil—
    May yet have shreds of dreams . . . small shreds of dreams.

Old Men in Gardening Time

Old men in garden season must forget
    The little span still left to shape their lives.
They make so much of time remaining yet,
    After a day for weeding rows arrives.

They turn the soil and plant and have an eye
    For winter stores, not knowing if they will
Be here to use the cellar stocks put by—
    Their only desire is to grub, to till.

Something of meadow mouse in all of these
    Old plodders, bending over plants and clod.
Something of mole and ant or frugal bees
    In old men taking seeds and breaking sod.

Oh, don't remind them! Let them have this hour—
    It soon will pass; let old men never know
How quick a sterner frost will blight each flower—
    How soon a killing wind will break each row.

Corn Belt Metropolis Notable

About his walk are hints of furrow-gait
    Sometime, somewhere a peasant forebear tilled
Good hill soil, and the fatness of that knoll
    Still shows its impact on this heavy soul.
But always in the blending of such bloods
    The softer things are killed.

He hates the ones who hold his grossness up
    To satire with their sharp pens or their paint,
But on his walls he hangs in massive frames
    Rich springtimes . . . tall oaks wearing autumn flames.
He tries with leather volumes to erase
    His coarse and earthy taint.

Of no avail . . . a hewer down of trees
    Begot his kind and left a potent mark.
Give him his flakes of silver . . . let him toy
    With bonds and dry goods, if it bring him joy;
No use to try to graft upon a swine
    The thin song of a lark.

Masters of Old Matsell Farm

The new master orders good grain sown
Close to the spot where, in his turf-locked cell,
The old master sleeps; good corn is grown
Upon this knoll. I heard the old one tell
Of deer and wildcats on the very place
Where the new master's summer house is built.
There is pride mirrored in this young one's face
When he points to better crops upon the silt.

The old master never seemed to care—
His plows were rusty and his cattle lean,
And great horseweeds lined the fences where
The new master keeps the margin clean.
The old master boasted of his sins—
The new master shows you sheep and bins.

Hill Woman's Dream After Drought

She knew the heavy weariness
    That never leaves the flesh.
Each year the soil gave less and less,
    And scourges came afresh.

Blight on the corn, and bug, and mole
    Combined to thwart all dreams—
To choke each thin song from the soul
    And blot all songful themes.

But one spring came; "This year; this year
    We'll plan to go," he said.
Yet even then the weather-fear
    Was there, high overhead.

A red sun burned; "We'll take the trip
    We talked of years ago."
The gray cloud rode, a giant ship,
    Over the fields below.

The gray clouds rode on silver sail—
    The gray fields, cracked from thirst,
And then came down the crystal hail
    Where the worm and mouse fed first.

The bins are yawning and the mow
    Is but an empty pit.
There's no talk of a journey now
    Nor any hint of it.

But stubborn fields are courted yet
    And coaxed and pampered still.
A hill wife never can forget
    The promise in a hill.

Herb Doctor

The rafters of his attic and the floor
    Of his littered workshop hold a strange array;
Great bound festoons of magic weeds and roots
    Which blend to banish ills of crumbling clay.

The hillsides keep no guarded secrets back
    But freely give their panaceas up
To one who claims such wealth of subtle skill
    For mixing bitter potions in a cup.

Even the pasture bog has potent things
    To rob a blighting fever of its flame—
Here is the blossom that can heal a wound
    And only certain wood folk know its name.

Only those souls who talk with owl and crow
    And know the jargon of the sly raccoon
Can choose the proper bark to purge the blood
    And gather it in favored signs of moon.

FIRSTBORN

Sound of a nervous hoof within the stable;
    An early crowing cock; a broodmare's squeal;
A white descending moon, and on the table
    The remnants of his lonely midnight meal.

His hounds returning from their night of baying
    Along the bayou's edge; his lamp burnt low;
No rain to spoil tomorrow's rounds of haying,
    But little signs that anyone would mow.

Now back, now forth, he walked; the dews were chilly
    Upon his coatless back; he heard the sound
Of whippoorwills along the creek where hilly
    Pasture wasteland spanned his meadow ground.

The corn land to the west was black and waving
    With heavy summer blades of promised crop,
And firewood near the house he had been saving
    Still stood, cone-shaped, a giant wigwam's top.

Fecund the land; oats ready for the binning
    And in the house the midwife's watchful eye
Waiting to find the signs of life beginning—
    Waiting to catch the firstborn's treble cry.

Waiting to see the dawn and have a reason
    To rouse the anxious, nodding, patient one,
Informing him the years would bring a season
    Where he could leave these scarred fields to a son.

Hoping his tired mate would cease her labors—
    Soon give another life to fight the soil,
So the midwife's tongue could tell the curious neighbors—
    Life; life; birth; death; green sod; more lives; more toil!

Drunken Landowner

He feels the breeze that fans the linden bloom
    And welcomes it against his throbbing head.
    His bleating herd is waiting to be fed—
He staggers with his lantern through the gloom.

The cock that greets the morning by its call,
    Mocking the sunrise with a beating wing,
    Flaps from its roost to watch this sodden thing
Scratch with his pitchfork in a littered stall.

Bleary of eye, he sees the calf and sheep
    Crunching their clover at the fodder rack,
    And with a leaden step he totters back
To rouse his sweat-marked horses from their sleep.

Under the sun of noon he plods along
    Blind to the sky's blue bowl which roofs his field—
    Only concerned with what his loam will yield—
Deaf to the mating vesper sparrow's song.

Watching with jealous eye the mouse and bug;
    Striving to coax the corn sprouts from the soil;
    Restless until the fruitage of his toil
Returns to mock him from an earthen jug.

Weather Prophet

Mare's tails are in the blue—beware of storm.
    It always rains when they are in the sky,
And when a mackerel cloud assumes that form
    Look out for hail to bruise the heading rye.

The moon is wet, a hunter's powder horn,
    Tilted exactly right to spill the rain.
This kind of weather is the worst for corn
    But just the thing for hay and smaller grain.

The spiders reinforce their webs—take care.
    And put a keg beneath the slanting eaves.
Look at the way the pump is sweating there—
    See how the silver maple turns its leaves.

I heard the red cock crow throughout the night—
    The pigs were carrying straw between their teeth—
In the northwest is not a hint of light
    And not a tiny start shows underneath.

Thatch well the oat stacks for the nighthawks scream—
    Nail a few shingles on your shattered roof.
Tomorrow you'll stay indoors to smoke and dream,
    While your plow horse stamps upon a restless hoof.

Oh, it is good to be in tune with skies
    And know the varied signs of fur and feather,
Guided by maple, moon, and buzzing flies
    In all mysterious witch-lore of the weather.

MASS FOR A TENANT FARMER

It's a good grave this clay has made—
    Is the place fitting? Yes; how well.
This same hillock has known his spade—
    Let it furnish his sleeping cell.

A clean song that thrush is singing.
    It suits, too, for this same hour.
He saw this bird take first winging
    Out of its nest in the hedge bower.

A burnished sun is suspended high.
    He was friendly with suns like these.
Close to here is his plot of rye—
    Yonder his grove of maple trees.

Here are neighbors to clutch the handles—
    These silver handles for calloused hands.
A plowman's son has lighted the candles—
    The singers are grubbers, possessed of lands.

Take him, clay, he was ripe for going—
    He fought you fairly, but now you win.
In spite of his sweating, his plowing, sowing—
    Open, hill soil, and then close in.

Husker

Stars still hung in the inky sky
    When I heard his wagon upon the road.
The price of corn may be low or high,
    But a husker must early have his load.

He must never relinquish faith in the soil.
    He must never breathe a prayer for a mammoth crop.
A man of the loam must trust and toil—
    A grower of corn must never stop.

I hear him calling his cattle in
    When the moon is riding above the knoll.
It was eight o'clock when he locked his bin—
    Oh, he is a weary, weary soul!

But, when tomorrow has given dawn
    He will strip the husks with his bleeding hands;
These are hallowed hillsides he labors on—
    These lands were his father's lands.

Rug Hooker

Endless arrays of dusty rainbow shreds—
    Fragments of attic cloth which hid a mouse;
A wild profusion of dim blues and reds—
    Garments which knew a gayer, happier house.

Colors a Magdalene delighted in;
    Hues that on Sunday's in a church aisle
Caused wagging tongues to whisper of her sin
    Because of the alien style.

Suit which a fighter wore; keep moving, hands;
    These were the garments of a son, long mute;
Oh, hurry fingers—he was used to bands!
    He marched before a flute.

Move swiftly, old gnarled fingers, weave the scheme
    Of colored birds from attic gathered cloth;
Not every poet can produce a dream
    From stuff left by the moth.

Along with bound festoons of thyme and sage
    There hang these ancient, cast-off, dusty things;
Like the canary which was in that cage,
    Something has lost its wings.

Everything in this house is shorn of song—
    Only the days have pinions left for flying;
Move on, old fingers; be not overlong—
    You, too, are dying.

Asylum Dance

I.

The screechy fiddle calls the dancers in;
Joy is not only for the favored few
Out in the bigger world; begin, begin,
You dying puppets, this night is for you
Whom the fates battered; some poor potter's hand
Must have gone palsied on this sodden clay;
But dance, dance, dance; you cannot understand
My shallow reasonings; dance and be gay.

Outside the acres spread and ripple far—
Some of these dancers once possessed a share
Of wide green pastures; now they own each star
In the broad firmament, aflicker there.
What are mere acres when a mad brain dreams
It owns the universe, each stars that gleams?

II.

Here one may rot or one may madly dance
And have a choice of many eerie things.
Look how these things which God has bungled prance
Like jumping jacks upon a score of strings!
Whine on your fiddle; jump you ragged so—
Morning will find you locked within your cell.
Ah, this is free enough for anyone!
How few can choose their play, their work, their hell.

Who are the mad ones? Who, I ask—the poor?
Are these the mad ones? Is this poverty?
Are they released when once they pass this door,
Or do they need the tears of you and me?
I cannot say and have my answer right—
I only know they dance and laugh tonight.

OCTOGENARIAN

He hunches by the stove and does not heed
The few philosophies that form the group.
Ripe on the bough, his soul will soon be freed
From that old body husk. His weary stoop
Speaks of the burdens he has carried long.
His hands are eloquent with veins and seams—
Such need not have philosophy or song:
When one is eighty he subsists on dreams.
On ancient memories can such a man
Feed day on day; what cares he for this hour?
Four score of years have formed his living span.
Eighty long summers he has seen in flower.
Old buried loves, old joys, and many tears—
A life is rich that lasts for eighty years.

FALSE PROPHETS

"The moon is wet," I heard a wise one say.
It's good to know a rain is on the way.

Better than saying that the moon is dry,
Even if no black cloud has found the sky.

This is a time of year one wants to hope,
For heat-hags have their revels on that slope.

I look in vain, I see no hint or sign,
And each day's hot winds wilt the pumpkin vine.

The stove-side men sit near the stove, long cold.
The gift of weather lore is for the old.

"See how the cottonwood turns up its leaves;
Bring out a tub to set beneath the eaves."

I see no sign of rain appearing yet,
But I am glad they say that moon is wet.

Night Musings

Down through the birches comes the tone of night—
The tinkling herd bells and the bleat of sheep.
I know these sounds will make the setting right
For dreams to flit across the screen of sleep.
How far away the city's rumble seems,
How good this autumn incense on the air.
Tonight I choose the fellowship of streams
And all those jeweled constellations there.

I do not love my city less because
I left her company to be with oaks.
I am not one to cavil at her laws
Or say she chokes me with her chimney smokes.
My city is the mistress of my choice—
But there are times I hate her tone of voice.

Heron at Sunset

Lately, the cows with bulging udders went
Along this row of ash; I yet can hear
The leader's bell. The day is nearly spent.
I know tomorrow will be hot and clear
Because the sun sank in a ruby cloud
Of evening mist. Now down the sky there goes
A heron to her roost; with scoldings loud
There follow three or four jet-feathered crows.

These dusky birds I watch for but a flash,
But that lone heron is a lovely thing.
I see her balance on a branch of ash,
And then the tints of sunset touch her wing.
Oh, what a pity I must move; now she
Sees man, her ancient enemy, in me.

SUNDAY

The preacher's voice droned on and on—
My restless eyes were watching her;
She seemed athirst for platitudes
And made a patient listener
Who sat and did not stir.

Her hands were red and kitchen-scarred.
"The world is for the low and meek"
I heard the stumbling parson say,
And then a feeble wave of red
Went creeping up her cheek.
"The humble they inherit all—
Theirs be the cattle and the lands."
She drank the hollow, booming words.
Between my stifled yawns, I watched
Her gemless, withered hands.

MORNING MISTS ON THE WAPSIPINICON

Evening brought by whippoorwills,
    Morning ushered in by thrushes;
Midnight brooding on my hills—
    Soft frog croonings in my rushes.

These few things I'll always keep;
    Always hold and ever cherish—
Man is sure of loam-locked sleep—
    Then his fragile dreams must perish.

But the magic of this dawn
    When these gray mists wrap my river;
When the spell of the night is gone
    And the lone birch stands aquiver.

Ghosts of Indian chieftains walk
    Indian lovers . . . old squaws humming;
There is grizzled sachem's talk—
    Then the sinewed arms start drumming.

Each soft mist-cloud is a soul,
    Wafted back to carry warning
To the dreamer on his knoll,
    Charging him to keep each morning.

Charging him to clutch these dreams
    Which shed colors at their leaving
When the ghost braves send their screams—
    When their fawn-eyed mates start grieving.

Such a cool grave for the rest
    Of a world-whipped, tired rover
Silver mist-clouds for his breast
    When his last black night is over.

III.
Drama

Folk Stuff

Story of the Play

Louise Grader and her friend, Alyce, both artists and instructors in a middle-west summer Art Colony, arrange a program of folk material in spite of the chaperon's dubious attitude. From their folk file index they draw a teller of folktales and a country fiddler and a dulcimer player. The fiddler and tale teller do their utmost to be quaint and type-y. The dulcimer player is a disappointment, being a young and handsome college man. While he and Louise go to get his dulcimer, the storyteller regales a group of young people with tall tales of snakes that become unjointed and of a man with bees in his stomach. It remains, however, for Louise and the young dulcimer player to give an unintentional and specific example of the oldest, most authentic, and most universal folk stuff in all the world.

Cast of Characters

LOUISE GRADER: (Art instructor). Pretty. Young. From 18 to 20. A trifle affected in an arty way. Wears a smock made of material having large futuristic floral design. Wears straw sandals but no stockings. Hair is done Mona Lisa style or with a coronet braid. Wears large gold hoop earrings.

ALYCE MORGAN: (Her friend, also instructor). Pretty. Blonde. A little plump. About 20. Sophisticated. Wears stylish sport outfit.

INEZ BLOOM: (Chaperon of the Art Colony). Tall, severe-looking. The typical chaperon. About 40. Wears plain dark dress with white collar and cuffs.

HORACE MINOR: (Old fiddler). Stooped and wizened. About 60. Dressed shabbily in old roomy trousers, a plain white shirt with no collar but with a brass collar button holding it together in front. Old-fashioned frock coat, perhaps. Smokes a corncob pipe. Carries bandanna handkerchief in his pocket.

JIM SAWYER: (Storyteller). About 50. Fat and jolly. Short. Wears a shabby suit of an ancient vintage, much too tight for him. Heavy gold watch chain across his stomach. Silver-rimmed glasses worn far down on his red nose. A number of lodge emblems on his coat lapel.

DICK HORGAN: (The dulcimer player). Young, handsome, tall, well-dressed in modern suit with nice shirt, good tie, well-polished shoes, etc. About 23 or 24.

BOB: (Student). About 18. Attractive-looking boy. White duck trousers, white sweater, and white duck shoes.

IRENE: (His friend). About 17 or 18. White linen dress and white shoes. Very attractive and modern.

STUDENTS AND GUESTS: (No lines. May use as many as desired). Men and boys wear slacks and sweaters, trousers and shirts open at the neck. One may wear a white flannel, blue serge coat outfit; another a light tan summer suit. Any suitable summer costume. Girls wear summer clothes. One may wear shorts, another riding breeches. One or two, plain colored smocks. Some wear slacks and sweaters. One a flowery print dress, others skirts and sweaters or summer suits and dresses. No two need be dressed alike, but all should be in clothes appropriate for summer.

The action takes place at a rural retreat in Iowa on the banks of the Mississippi River.

The scene is the parlor of the house occupied by the Mississippi River Art Colony.

The time is the present.

SCENE: *It is a large, old-fashioned room with a fireplace, Center at back, and Mid-Victorian furniture. The walls are done with modernistic paintings placed "artilly" here and there. Several pieces of rather badly done sculpture, also done in the "modern" manner, are shown at various vantage points about the room. A long settee is on the Left. It is filled with cushions. When the room crowds up, the students take the cushions and sit on the floor. Opposite this settee, across the room, Right, is a plain deal table with a plain wooden chair drawn up to it. On this table is a small box for cardboard files, a ledger and other office paraphernalia. Three chairs in front of fireplace up Center. Six camp chairs against walls in hall Right Center. Windows up Right and Left; doors Right Center back.*

AT RISE: MRS. INEZ BLOOM, *a tall, rather severe-looking woman of forty, conventionally dressed, is sitting at the table. Opposite her on the settee, recline* LOUISE GRADER *and* ALYCE MORGAN. *The former is pretty and young but rather affected in an "arty" way. She wears a hand-blocked linen smock, the design of which is large futuristic flowers. Her hair is done Mona Lisa style and she wears large "gold" circles in her ears. Straw sandals are on her feet. Her friend,* ALYCE MORGAN, *is a blond, pretty in a comfortable, plump way. She too is sophisticated but has more poise than* LOUISE. *She wears very stylish sport clothes.*

INEZ. I hope you girls are all prepared.

LOUISE. All set.

ALYCE. When do you expect them?

LOUISE. Almost any minute now.

ALYCE. You *did* get the old fiddler, didn't you?

LOUISE. Yes. And, my dear, you'll just adore him. He's *so* typical.

INEZ. But does he know any folk tunes?

LOUISE. *All* of them. He knows all of the folk tunes of this whole middle-western section *and* lots of chanteys and all the spirituals you could think of.

ALYCE. He must have got around a lot.

LOUISE. He is the pure wanderlust type.

INEZ. And the old chap with the folk stories—did he promise to come?

LOUISE. *(Effusively)* He'll be here with bells on and with bees in his stomach.

INEZ. Good heavens!

LOUISE. I mean, with the story of the man with bees in his stomach. And all about hoop snakes and joint snakes.

INEZ. I'm fairly frightened. I appreciate your good intentions and all that, but I must confess I don't like your wild scheme at all.

ALYCE. But the idea back of this whole colony is to use the indigenous material of the country itself.

LOUISE. Absolutely. We want to waken an art consciousness in this region by using the materials that lie close at hand. This part of the country has its own folktales, folk music, and its own folk craft.

ALYCE. And Louise is going to bring this graphically before our students here by flaunting the very stuff of the soil before their eyes. Aren't you, Louise?

LOUISE. You bet! That's why I invited these men of the hills here tonight.

INEZ. *(Who has been riffling through the cards in the box, now withdraws three)* Ah, yes. Here we have them. *(Reading from cards)* An old fiddler playing his folk tunes. That's Minor, Horace. Sawyer, Jim—a teller of folktales. And here we have a dul—oh, yes, a dulcimer player. Horgan, Dick—playing native music on his crude instrument.

LOUISE. *(Pleased)* That should impress these kids that the very air of these hills is pulsing with living material which awaits interpretation. *(She settles back with an air of satisfaction.)*

INEZ. That all sounds very fine, but we have a big responsibility in looking after these young people. I just wonder if their parents would consider contact with some of the rough elements of this section, culture. I'm worried. Art to most people is just painting.

LOUISE. You speak of culture in its narrower sense. I have, no offense, a wider conception of the world. How can a person be cultured in the full meaning of the term if he doesn't know the very souls of the simple people who live close to the soil?

ALYCE. I wouldn't worry, Mrs. Bloom. Louise's idea is pretty mild compared to some of the things she's cooked up in the past. It's harmless enough, I'm sure. But I'm afraid that we're in for an evening of boredom. Personally, I'm not so strong for this hillbilly stuff.

LOUISE. You want your culture all predigested like—like—a cow's cud or something.

ALYCE. I'd relax, Mrs. Bloom, if I were you. The worst that can happen is that the fiddler may show up with a fine cargo of dandelion wine onboard.

INEZ. *(Scowling at card)* Humph!

LOUISE. What?

INEZ. There's something questionable about the dulcimer player. At least there are two question marks after his name. *(Fixing* LOUISE *with her eye)* Who *is* the dulcimer player?

LOUISE. Why—*(Taking a long breath)*—er—why—the man who plays the dulcimer. Yes!

ALYCE. The question marks mean that biographical material is lacking. You see, he doesn't come from around here.

LOUISE. But I couldn't imagine a folk evening without a dulcimer player, so my old fiddler told me of one up at Kingston, and I wrote to him. My fiddler says that he's a young man but that he plays for dances and learned a whole repertoire of folk tunes because there seemed to be quite a demand for them. I told him to be on hand tonight. Not having heard otherwise, I assume he's coming.

ALYCE. Well, let's get ready. *(Gets up)* Now where do you want your folk-fakers to sit or stand?

LOUISE. Alyce, I wish you wouldn't sneer that way. It spoils the whole spirit of the thing. *(Gets up. Crosses upstage)* The country fiddler will stand here and play a few folk tunes and interpolate a few explanations.

INEZ. *(The dulcimer player is on her mind)* The dulcimer player! Does he sit or stand?

LOUISE. Both—sort of. I'll have him put one foot on this chair and rest the dulcimer on his knee while he speaks briefly of the origin of the instrument.

ALYCE. *(Moving about)* Then you'll have to have the storyteller stand over here to make good composition.

LOUISE. *(Carried away)* The teller of folktales will stand here and relate some of his simple earthy stories. I'll stand on this side and, Alyce, you stand there. Mrs. Bloom will sit by the door so that no one may leave the room during the recital.

INEZ. You told them to come early so that they could get their final instructions?

LOUISE. Yes. I'm sort of having a dress rehearsal. They're not used to appearing in public, you know.

ALYCE. Except when they appear at dances or something.

INEZ. Girls, I appreciate your enthusiasm, but I'm extremely dubious.

ALYCE. *(Impatiently and a bit sharply)* Naturally, you're dubious. You wouldn't be hired as a hostess and chaperon if you *weren't* dubious about everything.

INEZ. But if these young people entrusted to us for culture and—

LOUISE. Hush. I think I hear them coming. *(A man is heard blowing his nose offstage. Then there is a shuffling step.* LOUISE *goes to* L. *door and opens it. Enter the* OLD FIDDLER. *He is stooped and wizened, dressed very shabbily and smokes a corncob pipe. He carries a fiddle case under one arm. He enters awkwardly and then removes his hat.)* Oh, I'm so glad you've come. Here, let me take your hat and fiddle. *(She places these on the table.* INEZ *rises and* ALYCE *takes the chair from under her and places it up Center in the position they had agreed upon.)* Girls, this is our player of folk tunes. I don't even know his name. (INEZ *and the* FIDDLE PLAYER *answer simultaneously.)*

INEZ. On the card it says—

FIDDLE PLAYER. Minor is the—

LOUISE. *(Interrupting. Talks loudly to top their voices)* And I don't want to know it. I thought it would be ever so much more fun if these men who have so kindly offered to come tonight would be anonymous. They will therefore simply be: "Our Fiddler," "Our Storyteller," and "Our Dulcimer Player." Have a chair, Our Fiddler. *(She indicates the chair which was arranged for him upstage. He does not see her gesture and sits in the center of the settee.* INEZ *sits in the upstage* C. *chair.* ALYCE *gingerly sits on end of settee, and* LOUISE *takes a cushion and sits cross-legged on it on the floor before the* FIDDLER, *who smokes vigorously to conceal his embarrassment while the* WOMEN *stare at him.* LOUISE, *almost reverently.)* Won't you speak?

FIDDLER. *(Blows his nose with great gusto on a red bandanna handkerchief.*

Then clears his throat very formally and leans forward.) It's quite a piece down here from my house and it's stirred up my asthamy a little.

LOUISE. Oh, you poor man! Do you have asthma?

FIDDLER. Yes, quite a bit. That and kidney trouble are two things that bother me a good deal.

INEZ. Perhaps we shouldn't have put you to all this bother?

FIDDLER. Oh, that's all right. I'm better when I'm fiddlin'. The doctor says it's my age. He says most people my age has a touch of kidney trouble. *(Craftily)* I'm all right if I don't have to play too steady.

LOUISE. Well, now, while we're waiting for the others, can you tell us something about the tunes you're going to give us this evening?

FIDDLER. How's that?

ALYCE. Where did you learn them? How many do you know? *(He turns and stares with interest at her plump blondness.* INEZ *raises her eyebrows knowingly at* LOUISE, *who shrugs her shoulders.)*

FIDDLER. I can't hardly answer your questions, ma'am. I don't know just how many tunes I do know. I reckon about a hundred. I can't hardly tell you where I learned them neither. Mostly I picked 'em up at dances, I guess.

LOUISE. *(Disappointed)* Oh, I thought it was some sort of heritage.

FIDDLER. No, ma'am. I just picked it up from my Pap the way he did from his Pap before him. They played at dances. I heard Pap whistlin' these tunes when I was just a little shaver.

ALYCE. *(Effusively)* Really?

FIDDLER. Then, later on, I went with him to the dances. Maw, she always went with him.

INEZ. *(Perfunctorily)* How interesting!

FIDDLER. *(Stares at her a moment and then concludes her remark means nothing).* I'd stay up and watch 'em dance as long as I could, and then I'd go to sleep settin' in a corner, and they'd pick me up and carry me into one of the bedrooms and lay me on the bed, and there I'd snooze until toward morning.

ALYCE. How wonderful!

FIDDLER. Yes, ma'am, considerin' the noise went on. When the dance was over, they'd pick me up and take me home, and I wouldn't wake up until next mornin'.

LOUISE. That's thrilling! But how did you learn—

FIDDLER. When you hear tunes for years like that you soon get to playin' 'em on a fiddle yourself. (LOUISE *and* ALYCE *are pleased with him. Even* INEZ *is thawing slightly*).

LOUISE. Tell us the names of some of your tunes.

FIDDLER. Well, I can't remember all of 'em but there's "Money Musk," "Virginia Reel," "Old Zip Coon," "Speed the Plow," "Golden Slippers," "Nigger in the Woodpile," "The Mockin' Bird," "Irish Washerwoman," "Durang's Hornpipe," "Little Brown Jug," and a whole lot of others.

LOUISE. *(Jumping up; clapping her hands; whirling about)* Oh, how lovely! Girls, can't you just taste the tang of the soil in those quaint names? If someone doesn't write a great American opera some day and use the rhythms of these quaint Middle-western folk tunes as a background, I'm going to try it myself.

ALYCE. (*To* INEZ). My Lord! She can't even play a Jew's harp.

LOUISE. *(Running to the* L. *door)* I hear someone else. *(Opening door)* Oh, this is such a pleasure. (*Enter a fat countryman—*STORYTELLER—*same age as* FIDDLER. *He has made some attempt to dress up for the occasion. He has succeeded in making himself look a little ludicrous. He wears a shabby suit, much too small. A heavy gold watch chain. Silver-rimmed glasses, with the bridge far down on his nose, call attention to his nose, which is very red. A number of lodge emblems on his coat lapel.)* Girls! Our teller of folktales! (STORYTELLER *grins broadly and pumps the hand of each woman vigorously with a muttered "Pleased to meet you." Crosses to* OLD FIDDLER, *winks and grins at him; shakes hands and takes chair up* R.C., *which is very obviously shoved at him by* INEZ.)

ALYCE. Well, now, Louise, the students will be coming soon, so if you have any rehearsing to do, you'd better be getting it in.

LOUISE. Our storyteller needs no practice. I'm willing to vouch for him in the raw. I heard him tell some of his stories down at the grocery store evenings, and I think they're charming. But I'd like to find out something about our dulcimer player, though.

STORYTELLER. *(Scratching his head)* Well, Miss, I'm afraid you'll be a little disappointed in the dulcimer player, though.

LOUISE. *(Anxiously)* And why?

STORYTELLER. *(Shifting about awkwardly and crossing his legs)* Well, you see, Miss, a dulcimer player wasn't exactly easy to get. Then besides, you said to be sure he was a real "type" like this fiddler and me.

FIDDLER. First off, we had quite a time to figure out just what you meant by "types," but we finally made up our minds that what you really meant was fellers that was kind of freaky and old-fashioned like him and me.

STORYTELLER. Yes. And when it came to that, we was stumped. We couldn't think of only one chap in the whole neighborhood that played a dulcimer.

FIDDLER. And he was a long way from bein' a type, as you call 'em. Why, this dulcimer playin' chap has even been to college.

ALYCE. *(With great interest)* Oh, a *young* man.

LOUISE. Is he authentic?

STORYTELLER. Well, he's old Harve Horgan's boy, and Old Harve was the best dulcimer player up the Wapsie Tiger neighborhood.

FIDDLER. Made his own dulcimer, too.

STORYTELLER. Of course the kid learned to play from his dad. When he went off to college, he'd come back summers to Kingston, where his ma lived, and then he'd get out the old dulcimer and tune it up and play at Bowery dances and Harvest Home Picnics. He's kept in practice, all right. We got him to come tonight. He can't find one of these here quaint suits to fit him, Miss, but he can sure play hell out of that dulcimer.

LOUISE. Well, I suppose it's the best that can be done. I'm a little disappointed, though. *(KNOCK on the L. door.)*

FIDDLER. *(Grinning broadly and winking at the STORYTELLER, who is also grinning)* Now just hold your horses, Miss. Maybe you won't be so disappointed after all. *(Another and louder KNOCK).*

ALYCE. (*Goes to the L. door. Opens it and backs away in surprise at the sight of* DICK—*a tall, young, handsome, well-dressed man standing there)* Oh! Er—how do you do? Are you looking for someone?

DICK. For Miss Louise Grader. I'm to help out in a program of folk music, I believe. (LOUISE *and* INEZ *move toward him.* LOUISE *is overwhelmed by the handsome stranger.* ALYCE *is unable to conceal her admiration. Even* INEZ *beams.*)

LOUISE. Oh, how do you do? *(Extends her hand)* It is so good of you to come. I am sure you'll contribute a great deal to our evening. Won't you have a chair?

DICK. Yes, thanks. But not until I've met everybody. Of course, I'll heed the admonition in your note and remain anonymous, but here's two old friends. *(Crosses to the* TWO OLD MEN *and shakes hands.)*

STORYTELLER. Hello, Dick.

FIDDLER. Old Harve Horgan's boy. Well! Well!

LOUISE. *(Slightly ill at ease)* This is my friend, Miss Alyce Morgan. Alyce, this is the dulcimer player.

ALYCE. *(Gushing)* Our dulcimer player!

DICK. *(Holding her hand)* Alyce. A most appropriate name. *(Pause. Fervently)* A beautiful name. (ALYCE *writhes in ecstasy.*)

LOUISE. Inez Bloom, the hostess of our art colony.

DICK. *(Bending over Inez's hand)* You look just like my Aunt Margaret. *(She scowls and withdraws her hand.)* My youngest aunt. Funny for a husky fellow like me to have an aunt only twenty-two years old. (INEZ, *very pleased, gives him back her hand, which he shakes with feeling.*)

ALYCE. *(Who has already placed a chair next to the one standing up* C.*)* Will you sit here? *(Almost tenderly)* Dulcimer player? *(He goes to the* C. *chair.* INEZ *and* LOUISE *rush to get the chair next to his, but* ALYCE *already has it. The* WOMEN *seat themselves* L. *of* ALYCE.*)*

LOUISE. Now you must tell us something about your music.

DICK. There isn't much to tell. A dulcimer is simply a homemade substitute for a piano. It is used only for playing chords or for "seconding," we call it. Now I know all the tunes your fiddler plays, for we've played together at dances many times. He will be your main attraction. I simply play second fiddle, as it were—or rather second dulcimer it happens to be in this case.

LOUISE. *(With feeling)* Oh, how lovely! *(The* STORYTELLER *and* OLD FIDDLER *break into audible laughter. The* OLD FIDDLER *attempts to muffle his chortles with his huge bandanna. He breaks into a violent fit of asthmatic coughing.* ALYCE *and* INEZ *look at each other, worried. Then they look at* LOUISE. *But she is gazing, transfixed, into the eyes of* DICK. *He has risen and is standing close to her. They are entirely absorbed in each other).*

ALYCE *(With asperity)* Well, now it's time for the students to be coming in. *(Sweetly to* DICK) There's only about twelve of the younger people will be here tonight. It was our idea to have the stories first and then the folk music. After that, we can let the young people ask questions.

LOUISE. *(To* DICK) But where's your dulcimer?

DICK. *(Looking straight at her. Talking only to her)* I came up from Kingston on the Interurban. I wasn't sure just where your meeting was going to take place. Some said it would be at the Opera House in the village. That's near the depot, so I left my dulcimer there. I knew I'd have plenty of time to go back and get it.

INEZ. You can run back and get it, and we can start the other part of the program while we're waiting.

DICK. It will take me about ten minutes.

LOUISE. *(Never taking her eyes from his face)* But do hurry.

DICK. *(With a meaning glance at* LOUISE). I'd be glad if Miss Grader would walk along. I may be a little confused as to directions.

ALYCE. Why, I think Miss Grader will want to be here when the students arrive. I'll be glad to go myself, though.

INEZ. *(Looking from one to the other young* LADIES *with a scowl)* No. I think both of you will be needed here. I'll go. I know the road perfectly. (DICK *casts an appealing look at* LOUISE.)

FIDDLER. Seein's I can't play till he gets back, I'll go. *(Rises.)*

DICK. Sit down! Think of your asthma.

LOUISE. I'll go. I'm not especially needed here. Alyce, you can talk to the students when they arrive and get things under way. We won't be a minute. *(To* DICK) Come on the back way through the passage, so we won't meet any of the students. I want this to be a surprise. *(She opens a door upstage* R.C. *There is a three-foot passage which leads to the back door. In this passage, on either side,* making the lane quite narrow, are folded camp chairs, tennis rackets, etc. They exeunt and the door is closed. NOISE of approaching STUDENTS is heard.)

INEZ. (Looking at her wristwatch) They'd just have to be prompt at a time like this.

FIDDLER. (Rising. Making for R.C. door) Excuse me. Be right back.

INEZ. Here! Where are you—

ALYCE. Sh-h-h.

STORYTELLER. Won't be a second. (Follows FIDDLER out R.C. door just as STUDENTS stream in from L.)

(INEZ stands at R.C. door with a smile of greeting. Twelve YOUNG PEOPLE ranging in age from 17 to 20 enter noisily. They are in a rollicking, laughing mood and equally divided as to sex. They wear the usual summer clothes, soiled flannels, beach pajamas, knickers, overalls, etc. Some carry notebooks. One of the boys goes to the door of passageway and gets four camp chairs from therein. Four of the GIRLS sit on them. The rest sit on cushions on the floor. The BOYS arrange themselves near the GIRLS. They sit downstage Right and are turned three quarters in order to look upstage. ALYCE stands behind the chairs upstage. INEZ sits on the settee.)

ALYCE. Now, my friends, we have quite a treat in store for you. The aim of this institution is to produce indigenous work. Our theory is that all great art must have its root in the soil. Although you are primarily interested in painting and sculpture, we believe that poetry, the drama, music and all the allied arts must be made of the very warp and woof of the soil if its people are to endure. Now, we have secured for tonight a true teller of folktales and two players of folk music. We trust you will get some inspiration from this evening. (Is about to move to seat on settee when she notices that STORYTELLER and FIDDLER have not yet returned. She goes on with her talk after a concerted sigh from the YOUNG PEOPLE has made their boredom felt.) I have a dream that someone may some time collect the folk songs of this community and cause them to be written down into a great volume. I should not be surprised if some day a great native opera should arise from these tunes. (Here the STUDENTS break into loud and prolonged applause. The applause is for the TWO OLD MEN who have just opened the R.C. door. The OLD FIDDLER comes first, wiping his mouth with the back of his hand. The STORYTELLER follows, having a little difficulty forcing a bottle back into the hip pocket of his tight-fitting trousers. They stand there, petrified with surprise as they see all the faces turned in their direction. The STUDENTS think theirs is a planned "entrance." ALYCE thinks the applause is for her. She holds her hand up deprecatorily) These ideas are not altogether my own, but my colleague, Miss Grader, who has been called out for a few minutes but will return shortly, says—*(Here* INEZ *catches her eye and indicates the* TWO MEN. ALYCE *indicates the chairs upstage where they must sit. They sit.)* The first thing will be a series of folk stories. The storyteller whom we have chosen—I am indeed sorry that Miss Grader is not here to introduce these people, but she will return soon—is a man well versed in snake lore, and at least one of his tales will be a snake tale. *(The* YOUNG PEOPLE *laugh uproariously at the unintended pun.* INEZ *rises; scowls; looks toward the* R.C. *door for* LOUISE. *The* STORYTELLER, *flattered, bows.)* We will ask questions in tomorrow's class. Will you begin, Mr. Storyteller?

STORYTELLER. *(He crosses and uncrosses his legs several times. He is ill at ease but not frightened. He begins as* ALYCE *crosses to sit on settee, after first looking anxiously out through* R.C. *door)* As the young lady has said, I go in pretty much for snake stories. It hain't no wonder either, for I've had a good bit of experience with 'em. *(Here he, without realizing it, scratches his red nose. The gesture is unconscious.)* And I've heard many old-timers tell what they knowed about 'em. I always says, keep your ears open and your mouth shut and you'll learn a lot. So all my life around the saloons—er—er—I mean restaurants or the barbershops, I've kept my ears open. Well, some people don't believe they's such a thing as joint snakes. Well, they is and I've seen one. They can dispute it forever but that don't change it none. The joint snakes are there just the same, no matter how many smart-alecks dispute it. *(He pauses, waiting. The* STUDENTS, *feeling that something is expected, burst into hilarious applause).*

ALYCE. *(Icily)* As Miss Grader has not yet returned to instruct you, I suggest that you take notes to provide a basis for class discussion tomorrow. *(Perhaps* Two *turn back the pages of their notebooks. To* STORYTELLER) You may proceed.

STORYTELLER. I was about twelve years old. My mother and me was goin' out after raspberries. All at once we come along by an osage hedge. *(All the* STUDENTS *are listening very attentively now.)* Our dog rushed in under the hedge and come up with a long black snake. He shook the snake and shook him until the snake come unjointed and the pieces flew every way. Well, we went on and picked berries. And when we come back, the snake had got together and crawled away. That I see myself, and anybody can believe it or not just as they please. *(There is a subdued murmur among the* STUDENTS. *They turn to confer with each other in whispers. There is a ripple of laughter quickly suppressed. The* STORYTELLER *turns to the* FIDDLER *and he winks at him.)*

ALYCE. *(Rises; goes to* R.C. *door; opens it; looks out anxiously; closes door; returns; looks at* INEZ) As Miss Grader has not yet returned and as the musical program can't be taken up until she gets back, I'm wondering if our Storyteller couldn't give us another of his charming folktales.

STORYTELLER. *(With pride)* Yes, ma'am!

OLD FIDDLER. I'm going out a minute, Miss. I'll be right back. *(Exits R.C. door.)*

ALYCE. *(With a flourish of her hand toward the STORYTELLER)* And now! Mister Storyteller! *(She sits.)*

STORYTELLER. Well, another story that people have always liked to hear me tell is the one about the fellow over by McCausland who had the swarm of bees in his stomach.

IRENE. Oh, my Lord!

STORYTELLER. There was a fellow by the name of Knowles live over on the Wapsie Bottoms, and he's had a pain in his stomach for thirty years. He'd tried everything—chiropractors, osteopaths, faith doctors, Christian Science, patent medicine, electric belts, Indian herbs, liquor—*(Pauses. Fetches up a sigh of longing)*—every common medicine doctor from Clinton to Keokuk, Ioway. And he'd been to Chicago twice. "You got to die," they all said. "You got cancer." He was just a skeleton. He couldn't eat nothin'—*(There is a SOUND at the R.C. door.)*

ALYCE. *(Rises to her feet)* Ah, Miss Grader and the dulcimer player at last. *(Door opens and the OLD FIDDLER enters R.C. sheepishly. Closes door carefully behind him. Winks at STORYTELLER, who glares at him.)*

STORYTELLER. As I was about to say when I was interrupted— (OLD FIDDLER *is subdued.)* He couldn't drink nothin'—I *mean,* eat nothin'. He hadn't done a tap of work for years, and nights the neighbors could hear him screamin' from pain. Finally, when he'd give up, he heard of Old Doc Cook up at Toronto. Doc Cook was known as one of the best doctors in the country when you could ketch him sober. Old Doc Cook was fairly sober when this fellow got there. "How long you been this way?"—Doc says. "Thirty years," the fellow told him. "What did you eat the day before you first noticed the pain—thirty years ago?" Doc asks him. "Warm biscuits and honey," the fellow says. "Just what I thought," Doc says. "Comb honey, too, wasn't it?" "Yes," the fellow says. Doc was already mixin' up some medicine. "What's the matter with me?" the fellow asks. "You et bee eggs with that honey," Doc says. "You've had a swarm of bees in your stomach all these years!" *(He pauses impressively and looks around. He clears his throat and proceeds)* "I'll give you a dose of sulfur and then some whiskey to dissolve the sulfur. They kill bees with sulfur, you know. Don't you worry. I'll bring you out." *(Pause.)* He did, too. The fellow's well and hearty today. *(A gale of laughter greets the close. The OLD FIDDLER laughs so heartily that he is seized with a coughing spell. The STORYTELLER is very pleased. Everyone is smoking now, the OLD FIDDLER'S pipe sending up blue wreaths. ALYCE and*

INEZ *look at each other. They are worried about* LOUISE.)

INEZ. *(Rising)* If our storyteller will favor us with one more story—*(An involuntary groan rises from the* STUDENT *body. It is quickly suppressed by a patter of applause. One of the boys rises from the floor and leans over to whisper to a girl.)* I will go and see what has detained Miss Grader. I am sure I will be gone only a moment. We are unable to go on with our musical program until Miss Grader returns. Miss Morgan will say a few words—

ALYCE. Crude as these little folktales are—

STUDENT. *(The* BOY *who has been leaning over the* GIRL'S *chair)* Pardon me, Mrs. Bloom. But we thought we would all be more comfortable if we had more camp chairs. So Irene and I—*(The* GIRL *springs eagerly to her feet and stands next to him. They hold hands.)* thought that we'd go out and bring some in.

INEZ. You'll do nothing of the sort. Sit down, Bob. Irene! *(They sit, pouting. The other* STUDENTS *make faces of derision at them.)* If any chairs are needed, I will get them. Who wants a chair? (ALL *sitting on the floor raise their hands.)* Very well. Continue, Miss Morgan. *(While* ALYCE *speaks,* INEZ *goes to* R.C. *door to get chairs from passage. She opens door a trifle so that she can see out, but not the audience.)*

ALYCE. All great literature is tinged with the stuff of these simple folk narratives. Now if our STORYTELLER —*(She stops as* INEZ *closes door and gasps loudly)* Why, what—

INEZ. *(Is upset, but pulls herself together and crosses to where* ALYCE *is standing, next to* STORYTELLER *and* FIDDLER) Attention! Because of something that has unexpectedly occurred, it becomes necessary to dismiss you. You will please all leave at once and ask no questions. Leave by the west door. All classes will meet tomorrow as usual. Please lose no time in leaving. *(Her tone is so authoritative that they leave abruptly by the* L. *door. The* STORYTELLER *and the* FIDDLER *are bewildered. They remain in their places. When the last* STUDENT *has gone,* INEZ *motions them also toward the* L. *door.)*

STORYTELLER. But don't you want no more earthy stories?

INEZ. Please go.

FIDDLER. But I ain't played yet.

INEZ. We'll have no more use for you this evening. *(They exeunt* L. *in some bewilderment and head-shaking and many a backward glance.)*

ALYCE. *(When they are alone)* What in Heaven's name has happened? *(WARN Curtain.)*

INEZ. Louise wanted this folk stuff, didn't she, and you, too.

ALYCE. Yes, but—

INEZ. I thought I was ignorant—being only the chaperon—didn't know what genuine folk stuff was. But I've come upon as fine an example of it tonight as I ever expect to see in all my days.

ALYCE. *(Afraid of her strange manner. Looks at her)* Did you come across some primitive drama?

INEZ. Primitive is right. *(Her manner is demoniacal)* I have seen the beginning of all folklore in the world; the unbridled folk stuff that lives close to the soil—It's simple, quaint, earthy and absolutely uninhibited—the most utterly natural thing you've ever heard of.

ALYCE. If you will report your findings to the students in class tomorrow—

INEZ. *(Ironically)* The students will stumble upon it themselves in time—those that have not already experimented with it.

ALYCE. *(Bewildered and a little offended)* Is there any reason why *I* should not know of this new folk material that you have unearthed?

INEZ. None in the world, my dear. *(Goes to* R.C. *door; puts hand on knob. With the air of an oracle)* I am about to show you the oldest, best known, and most authentic folk stuff in all the world. *(She throws the door wide open.* LOUISE *and* DICK *are seen, locked in each other's arms, standing in the passageway. They are profile to audience. Both her arms are about his neck. His upstage arm (left) encircles her waist. Under his downstage arm he carries the dulcimer. He does not see the two* WOMEN *staring at them.* LOUISE *does, and hurriedly puts her two hands on either side of his face so that he sees nothing. He starts to put his right arm about her. The dulcimer slips to the floor with a "ping-ga-ping" as both his arms go tightly around her.* INEZ, *triumphantly)* Try and get *that* into a lecture with slides.

QUICK CURTAIN

Index

Anamosa, Iowa, 6
Anderson, Sherwood, vii, 1, 6, 8, 10, 14
Andrews, Clarence, 10

Berry, Wendell, 15
Blunden, Edmund, 8, 9
Burroak and Sumac, 14

Cedar Rapids Gazette, 4, 6, 9, 12
Cedar Rapids Republican, 5, 13
Coe College, 12–13
Cone, Marvin, 11, 12
Cornell College, 8, 11

Des Moines, Iowa 14
Des Moines Register, 9, 14, 15
Duncan, Thomas W., 14

Eliot, T. S., 5, 6
Engle, Paul, 3, 5, 7, 10, 11, 12, 15

Ferreter, Edward, 2, 3, 6, 7, 8, 13
Finger, Charles, 8, 9, 10, 13
Folk Stuff, 7, 102
Frederick, John T., 8, 10, 11

Gorge Rapids, 23, 24, 30–33, 36
"Grant Wood Meets Jay G. Sigmund," 3, 6

Hemingway, Ernest, 2, 6, 14

Jeffers, Robinson, 1, 8, 9

Kooser, Ted, 5

Lake Woebegone, 10
Least of These, The, 4, 13, 14

Masters, Edgar Lee, vii, 2, 3, 14
Midland, The, 10
Minnesota Mutual Life, ix, 2, 4

O'Brien, Edward J., 2, 14
Ontarns, 14, 30, 31, 33, 39, 43, 49

Regionalist, 1, 2, 3, 14
Ridge Road, 31, 40, 82, 83
Ridge Road, The, 9

Sandburg, Carl, vii, 1, 3, 8, 14
Sigmund, Jay G.: Cedar Rapids, Iowa, and vii, 1, 2, 3, 4, 6, 9, 11, 12, 13; death of 11–13; insurance career of vii, 2–5, 12; nature and vii, 4, 9, 11, 12, 15; neighborliness and vii, 3, 5, 12, 14, 15; reviews of 2, 4, 8, 9, 10, 14, 15
Smith, Betty, 3, 4, 8
Stein, Gertrude, 2, 8
Stevens, Wallace, 2, 5
Stone City, Iowa, 7, 11

Tolstoy, Ilya, 1, 9

Vine Leaves, 3–4

Wapsipinicon, vii, 2, 6, 10, 13, 14, 15–16, 21, 30, 31, 36, 39, 45, 49, 98
Wapsipinicon Tales, 9–10
White, Roland A., 4, 14
Williams, William Carlos, 2, 5
Winesburg, Ohio, 8, 10
Wood, Grant, 3, 5–7, 14

About the Editor

Zachary Michael Jack was born on his family's one-hundred-and-fifty-year-old Iowa Heritage Farm. His advocacy of place studies includes service as founder-director of the Iowa School of Lost Arts for children, advisory boardmember of the Interversity Place Studies listserv, and consulting editor of the series *Voices from the American Land* edited by environmental journalist and policymaker Charles E. Little. The author of two place-based collections of poetry, *The Inanity of Music and Wings* and *Perfectly Against the Sun*, Jack is an assistant professor of English at North Central College, where he teaches courses in writing and rural studies.

A fourth-generation Iowa farmer's son and great-grandson of the farm conservation writer Walter Thomas Jack, Zachary Michael Jack has authored or edited many books, including several previous collections on rural life and letters: *Love of the Land: Essential Farm and Conservation Readings from an American Golden Age*; *Black Earth and Ivory Tower: New American Essays from Farm and Classroom*; and *The Furrow and Us: Essays on Soil and Sentiment*. *Black Earth and Ivory Tower* and *The Furrow and Us* have been nominated for the Theodore Saloutos Award for the year's best book on agricultural history. Jack has presented his research on place-based writing at the Society for the Study of Midwestern Literature, the Agricultural History national conference, and the Newberry Seminar for Rural History, among many others.

www.ingramcontent.com/pod-product-compliance
Lightning Source LLC
Chambersburg PA
CBHW021410290426
44108CB00010B/463